TAYLOR
SWIFT

ALSO BY LOUISA JEPSON

Harry Styles: Every Piece of Me

TAYLOR SWIFT

Louisa Jepson

**SIMON &
SCHUSTER**

London · New York · Sydney · Toronto · New Delhi

A CBS COMPANY

First published in Great Britain by Simon & Schuster UK Ltd, 2013
A CBS COMPANY

Copyright © 2013 by Louisa Jepson

1 3 5 7 9 10 8 6 4 2

Simon & Schuster UK Ltd
1st Floor
222 Gray's Inn Road
London WC1X 8HB

www.simonandschuster.co.uk

Simon & Schuster Australia, Sydney
Simon & Schuster India, New Delhi

A CIP catalogue record for this book is available
from the British Library

Hardback ISBN: 978-1-47113-087-8
Trade Paperback ISBN: 978-1-47113-088-5
eBook ISBN: 978-1-47113-090-8

Typeset in the UK by M Rules
Printed and bound by CPI Group (UK) Ltd, Croydon, CR0 4YY

PROLOGUE

'It's nice to meet you.
I'm Taylor'

The lights faded and the noise reached dizzying levels as screams, whistles and cheers blurred into a cacophony of sound. The word RED illuminated the stage, before neon letters spelling TAYLOR SWIFT scrolled past. 'Tay-lor, Tay-lor, Tay-lor.' The chants echoed around the arena, as the fans went crazy.

Suddenly the singer's dark, willowy silhouette became visible behind a silky scarlet curtain and she burst into the rocky hit 'State of Grace', accompanied by a seven-piece band, four backing singers and fourteen dancers. As she reached the chorus, the screen dropped and disappeared. Dressed in tiny black hotpants, a white lacy shirt, a black hat and red shoes, Taylor looked out to the sea of people all shouting her name and gave an awestruck red-lipstick-stained smile. Her green eyes crinkled with delight, enjoying the perfect moment.

The sold-out Omaha arena was full of bright, colour-coded accents: the red on Taylor's shoes matched the ones on her microphone and on the banners, bows, headbands and glowsticks held up by her army of followers, who hung on her every word.

As the anthem finished with a flourish, Taylor tossed her hat into the enormous throng of fans and threw her loosely curled blonde hair to one side. She paused for a split second. This was the moment she had been waiting for: the opening night of her worldwide Red tour. It had been seven months in the pipeline and had involved long days in rehearsals, hundreds of hours of planning and an enormous team of people to bring her vision to life.

'Well, good evening,' she told the crowd. 'You see, this is the part I've been really looking forward to for a very long time because this is the part where I say to you, Omaha, Nebraska, welcome to the very first night of the Red tour.'

She listened to the applause with delight and smiled again, blinking back tears of happiness.

'Thank you for coming tonight, first of all,' she continued. 'If I have seen you before – which I might have because we really like playing in Omaha – it's good to see you again. If I haven't seen you before it's nice to meet you. I'm Taylor.'

As her fans knew, Taylor's unswerving devotion to them and to storytelling was always going to be at the heart of her new show.

'I write lots of songs about my feelings,' she continued.

'I'm told I have a lot of feelings. So by you being here tonight, all 13,500 of you have opted into hearing me sing songs about my feelings for the next two hours. So thank you for that . . .

'The way I see emotions in my head, I compare them to colours: for me blue is sad, yellow is comfort and warm. There is one colour that defines a lot of the emotions I have written about lately: emotions like frustration, anger, jealousy, falling in love, falling out of love, heartbreak – all that good stuff. You know, I wrote about all that stuff so much that I even named an entire album after it. I maybe even went so far as to name an entire world tour after it. Ladies and gentlemen, boys and girls, the colour that defines the emotions that shape us and teach us things, I think there's one colour that represents the most important ones. And that colour is red.'

Her euphoric fans brought the house down with their cheers and Taylor drummed her way through 'Holy Ground', before blasting the title track, 'Red', and the popular 2008 hit, 'You Belong to Me'.

Thirteen of the seventeen songs in the resplendent two-hour set came from her new album and the show featured as many costume changes for the dancers as for Taylor herself. One swap took a record four and a half seconds according to the singer's mum, Andrea, dubbed Momma Swift by Taylor's supporters.

There were also numerous set changes involving pyrotechnics and hydraulics, although the scenes were less fantastical than those seen at her previous sell-out gigs.

She told ABC: 'I think that the visuals portrayed on this tour will be, I guess, more grown-up and a little bit more mature than things we've done in the past. I think on my previous albums and my previous tours, I've really liked to operate in the element of fantasy, and I think that this tour incorporates a little bit more reality into the visuals, which is nice.'

It was still a visual delight for her audience. During 'Love Story', her dancers dressed as wind-up dolls wandering out of a white music box in a dreamlike scene; there were rodeo-style stage props for 'Stay, Stay, Stay'; and Taylor recreated 1940s Hollywood glam for 'The Lucky One'. At one point, there was a montage of pictures of the singer over the years, taken from family videos of her at nearly every age from one to twenty-two: being held by her parents; receiving a guitar at Christmas; singing the National Anthem; and performing old songs. When the count reached twenty-two, the pop-country superstar took the stage with her dancers to appropriately perform her anthem, '22'.

Singer/songwriter Ed Sheeran, who had opened the show, also joined her on stage for their sweet duet, 'Everything Has Changed'. Other highlights included a dubstep rendition of 'I Knew He Was Trouble', Taylor being suspended in the air during 'Sparks Fly' and a touching and powerful rendition of the wistful ballad 'All Too Well' on a ruby-red grand piano. During the course of the show, the talented star also played the electric, acoustic and 12-string guitars and the banjo.

The grand, carnival-themed finale, 'We Are Never Ever Getting Back Together', saw Taylor become the ringmaster flying above the audience in a circus–sized production, surrounded by fireworks, stilt walkers and clowns, topped off with a blizzard of ruby-red confetti.

'Please, never get back with your horrible exes,' Taylor advised.

Taylor's magnificent production sums up everything she has achieved in her twenty-three years: more than most professional musicians will manage in an entire lifetime. With record sales in excess of 26 million albums and 75 million song downloads worldwide, Taylor is one of the hottest acts on the planet. Her tenaciousness and sheer determination is almost unheard of in a world where many artists have overnight success through talent shows and disappear after one or two albums. Taylor isn't going anywhere; her success just seems to grow by the day.

The triumph of her most recent album, *Red*, made her the first artist since the Beatles and the only female artist in history to log six or more weeks at No. 1 with three consecutive studio albums and she is the only female artist in music to twice have an album hit the 1 million first-week sales figure. Taylor is *Billboard*'s youngest-ever Woman of the Year, holds the record for the most songs to debut in the Top 10 of the *Billboard* Hot 100 and also boasts the Hot 100 record for most songs by a female artist in the chart in a single week. She is also a seven-time Grammy winner, and is the youngest recipient in history of the music industry's highest honour, the Grammy Award for Album of the Year.

Combined with her incredible talent for catchy melodies is her girl-next-door openness and expressiveness about her emotions surrounding her relationships. She has captured the imaginations of hundreds of thousands of youngsters across the globe and is the ultimate girl's girl.

'Fans are my favourite thing in the world,' she said. 'I've never been the type of artist who has that line drawn between friends and their fans. The line's always really blurred for me. I'll hang out with them after the show. I'll hang out with them before the show . . . Who am I to think I'm better than talking to people.'

Taylor may have started out as a dreamy 11-year-old walking up and down Music Row in Nashville handing out her CD and hoping someone would offer her a record deal, but life in the fast lane has not changed her.

'I'm not a big deal,' she said to *The Times*. 'I am the same person that sat there in ninth grade, I still have insecurities, things I doubt about myself, I still have frustrations, things that confuse me. I just look at it that I have a different schedule now, I love people, and personal conversations. If we were sitting here right now and I was all guarded and twisted about what you might ask me, and paranoid about the way people view me, I'd be putting myself in such a cage. It's so much easier to like people, and let people in, to trust them until they prove that you should do otherwise. The alternative is being an iceberg.'

It's this connection that makes Taylor so adored by her followers, who understand her words and feelings.

She told the *Guardian*: 'I think that we all have our memories, and our hope for future memories. I just like to hopefully give people a soundtrack to those things.'

Taylor's Red tour is still on the road in North America and will travel to Australia and New Zealand in November 2013. Taylor is only listening out for one thing:

'When you're singing you can hear the echo of people in the audience singing every single word with you, and that was that big dream that I had for myself,' she said. 'It's happening.'

CHAPTER ONE

'I was infatuated with the sound, with the storytelling'

In the 1960s, a pretty young American woman was forging her career as a professional opera singer. With cut-glass blue eyes, a full smile and high-arched eyebrows, she bore a striking resemblance to one of the biggest female stars in the world today. The performer's name was Marjorie Finlay. She was Taylor Swift's grandmother.

Taylor's mum, Andrea Gardner Finlay, grew up sitting backstage in bustling concert halls or on the gilded front row of theatres, watching wide-eyed as her mother sang the lead roles in classic operas and iconic musicals such as *The Bartered Bride*, *The Barber of Seville* and *West Side Story*. Marjorie lived a nomadic lifestyle, travelling alongside her husband Bruce, an engineer, who moved around the world as an oil-rig worker, and took jobs where she could. She was

1

bewitching and captured attention wherever she performed.

'I have these gorgeous, glamorous pictures of her in black-and-white,' Taylor told *Rolling Stone*. 'She was just so beautiful. Wherever my grandfather would go for his engineering job, my grandmother would go and perform and sing opera. She was in all these musicals in Singapore and all these gorgeous places where my mum grew up. My mom has these amazing stories of growing up overseas, and then she moved to America when she was about ten.'

Marjorie was clearly a gutsy and strong woman who was happy to take risks to get ahead in her career.

'In Puerto Rico, my grandmother was the hostess of a top-rated TV variety show called the Pan American show,' Taylor told *Wood & Steel* magazine. 'Her Spanish was so bad that the Puerto Ricans thought she was hysterically funny! She went on to become the "madrina" [symbolic grandmother figure] of the air force. They really loved her!'

The Finlays eventually settled in the vibrant city of Houston in Texas and, later, Andrea met Scott Kingsley Swift – who came from Pennsylvania – while he was visiting her hometown on a business trip. After a whirlwind romance, the couple married on 20 February 1988 in Harris County, Texas, and settled in the small town of West Reading in Pennsylvania. Not long after making roots into their new home, Andrea fell pregnant with their first child. Taylor was already listening to music in the womb but, rather than the serene classical music of Bach and Mozart that many pregnant women favour, Andrea tuned into her favourite hard-rock quartet, Def Leppard.

'My mom was a huge fan of theirs when she was pregnant with me,' Taylor told MTV.

Taylor Alison entered the world on 13 December 1989 in Reading Hospital in Wyomissing, Pennsylvania. The new parents fell in love with their tiny daughter instantly.

Like his father and grandfather before him, Scott worked as a stockbroker for the large financial firm Merrill Lynch, and Andrea also worked in finance. The couple decided on the name Taylor, after the American singer-songwriter James Taylor, because they thought the gender-neutral name might help her get ahead in her career, should she follow in her parents' footsteps.

The singer explained to the *Toronto Star*: 'She named me Taylor so that if anybody saw on a business card the name, Taylor, they wouldn't know if it was a girl or a guy if they were thinking of hiring me.'

Thirteen might be an unfortunate number for some but Taylor has always viewed it as her lucky number because of her birthday, telling the *Daily Mail*: 'I was born on December 13. I was 13 when I got my first record deal and my Twitter name is taylorswift13. My first single, 'Tim McGraw', had a 13-second intro, and every time something good happens, 13 is involved. If I ever get a tattoo it will be 13.'

Taylor had something special about her from the first day and Andrea admits that even at a few hours old her little girl's distinctive personality shone through.

In the TV documentary *Teen Superstar*, she marvelled: 'Taylor was maybe a few hours old and a paediatrician said, "She's a really good-natured baby but she knows exactly what she wants and how to get it." I thought, "What is this guy on?" But he just gave me a very interesting description of her which absolutely fitted her to a tee.'

Like a lot of new mums, Andrea's career took a back seat and she decided to quit her job to stay at home to look after her new baby daughter.

'Before she had me, she was a really big business executive that worked at an ad agency,' Taylor told cable channel Great American Country (GAC). 'I really look up to that. She had me when she was thirty. She had a complete career of her own and was supporting herself.'

Taylor was always happy that she had her mum around and Andrea instilled values of independence and spirit, just as Marjorie had done for her when she was a child.

'My mum decided to stay at home to raise me,' Taylor said to the *Ottawa Citizen*. 'She totally raised me to be logical and practical. I was brought up with a strong woman in my life and I think that had a lot to do with me not wanting to do anything half way.'

The Swifts' first-born had blonde corkscrew curls and a huge smile and people always commented on what a gorgeous baby she was. As soon as Taylor was talking, she was trying to drum up an audience to listen to her.

'My parents have videos of me on the beach at, like, three, going up to people and singing *Lion King* songs for them,' she told *Marie Claire* magazine. 'I was literally going from towel to towel, saying, "Hi, I'm Taylor. I'm going to sing 'I Just Can't Wait to Be King' for you now."'

There is also home footage of the little girl singing a

particularly hard song to master, the Righteous Brothers' 'Unchained Melody', aged just two. Like most young children, Taylor adored the sparkling magic and fairytales of Disney movies and if she forgot the words to her favourite films, she would just make them up. Remarkably, she even recalled the entire musical soundtrack to one film after seeing it just once.

'I would come out of Disney movies singing the entire songs, and my parents were like, "Didn't you just hear that once?"' she said to Country Music Television (CMT) news. 'So I think that was my first real comprehension of the fact that music was what I remember the most from a movie. Not exactly the plotline as much as the music.'

Taylor explained to chat-show host Oprah Winfrey: 'My whole life I've loved music. I would see all these people on big stages and I didn't think I could do that . . . I just loved music.'

She also had a chance to belt out hymns in church. The Swifts were devout Catholics and Taylor would accompany her family to church and go to Sunday School. She vividly recalls her grandmother's stunning voice.

'I can remember her singing, the thrill of it,' Taylor said to the *Reading Eagle*. 'She was one of my first inspirations.'

Talking to *The Australian*, she mused: 'She would have these wonderful parties at her house, and she would get up and sing. She always wanted to be on stage, whether she was in the middle of her living room or in church. She just loved it. And when she would walk into a room, everyone would look at her, no matter what. She had this thing, this it-factor.

I always noticed it, that she was different from everyone else.'

On 4 March 1993, her little brother Austin was born and Andrea had her hands full, looking after two bright young children. By then, Taylor had started attending nursery school and then pre-school at the Alvernia Montessori School, which was run by nuns.

The school's head, Sister Ann Marie Coll, told the *Reading Eagle*: 'She was kind of shy but not too shy, and she always liked to sing. When she was in grade school, she came back and played guitar for the children.'

When she was very small, Taylor befriended another pretty blonde girl called Brittany Maack, who later inspired her song 'Me and Britney'.

Brittany told the *Reading Eagle*: 'When I first met Taylor, we were a couple of months old. We grew up together from babies, to toddlers, to teenagers. We were more sisters than friends. Taylor's family was my family ... Taylor was extremely smart growing up. She looked at things almost with what I would call an old soul, but she had such an amazing imagination.'

Taylor was able to foster her imagination on a picturesque 15-acre Christmas-tree farm in rural Montgomery County where she grew up. She describes it as 'the most wonderful place in the world'. Her parents weren't farmers but they loved the idea of bringing their children up in the great outdoors and Andrea ran the family's small business selling Christmas trees every December.

The family owned several Quarter Horses and a Shetland

pony called Ginger. Taylor was first sat on a pony when she was nine months old and horse-riding later became one of her favourite hobbies. After school and during weekends and school holidays, she would race home to spend her free time hitching a ride on the farm tractor with her brother, Austin, sitting in the hayloft, exploring the endless countryside on her pony and picking fruit in the sunny orchard.

Speaking to *Philadelphia* magazine, she said: 'I used to walk everywhere barefoot. It was the most magical, amazing way to grow up.'

Her earliest job, long before she was living the glamorous life of a superstar, was picking praying mantis eggs off trees so they didn't start hatching in people's homes.

During an interview with Jay Leno on *The Tonight Show*, Taylor revealed: 'I was too young to help with the hauling of the trees up the hills and putting them onto cars. So, it was my job to pull off the praying mantis pods from Christmas trees. I forgot to check one time and they hatched all over these people's houses. There were hundreds of thousands of them. And they had little kids and they couldn't kill them because that'd be a bad Christmas.'

As well as horses, the family had a number of semi-feral barn cats. At night, they would hunt and kill stray rodents and birds. According to Andrea, whenever Taylor woke up and saw the dead animals on the driveway, her exceptional imagination would be sparked and she would make up stories about what had happened to them.

'Taylor would literally start to create little conversations and storylines involving all these dead animals on the drive-way,' Andrea remembered.

As well as being unusually creative, Taylor was vivacious and gregarious, qualities her parents embraced and encour-aged. When people came to the farm, Taylor would charm them with her confidence and engage everyone she met in conversation.

'I think I fell in love with words before I fell in love with music,' she told Katie Couric's *'All Access' Grammy Special*. 'All I wanted to do was talk and all I wanted to do was hear sto-ries. I would drive my mum insane . . .'

She wasn't always talking; sometimes they would sit back and observe people together.

Andrea added: 'From day one, Taylor was always trying to figure out how other people thought and what they were doing and why they were doing it. That was probably an early telltale sign that she had the makings of a songwriter.'

Unlike most youngsters, Taylor was very rarely naughty and in many ways, as her friend Brittany noted, she was old before her time; an attribute she still possesses to this day.

'When I was naughty as a kid, I used to send myself to my own room,' Taylor explained to the *Daily Mail*. 'My mum says that she was afraid to punish me sometimes because I was so hard on myself when I did something wrong. I haven't changed much since then. I live half my life in the present and half of it as an 80-year-old grandmother . . .'

When she was aged six, Taylor was given her first album, LeAnn Rimes's *Blue*. LeAnn was one of the biggest teen country stars of all time and had released the album when she was just thirteen years old. She went on to become the first country artist to ever receive the hailed Best New Artist Grammy Award. Taylor listened to her new album non-stop, learning all the words to the songs off by heart. LeAnn was her new idol.

'LeAnn Rimes was my first impression of country music,' she told the *Guardian*. 'I just really loved how she could be making music and having a career at such a young age.'

When she was eight, she managed to get tickets to see LeAnn Rimes in a concert at Atlantic City. She told *Philadelphia Style Magazine* (also known as the *Philly*): 'I was totally freaked out. Seeing this person who was my hero . . . it was crazy.'

After discovering LeAnn, Taylor traced the history of country music back in time and listened to older artists like Dolly Parton and Patsy Cline, humming along to their songs in her bedroom.

In the long summer holidays, the Swifts would go to their holiday home in Jersey Shore, on a picturesque bay in Stone Harbour, which her parents bought when Taylor was just two.

'I was there every summer, all summer for the majority of my childhood,' she told the *Philly*. 'It was such an amazing way to grow up. There were so many places to explore, whether it was finding a new island in the inlet or walking to 96th Street for ice cream. I could not have had a cooler childhood.'

She added to *Vogue*: 'That's where most of my childhood

memories were formed. We lived on this basin where all this magical stuff would happen. One time, a dolphin swam into our basin. We had this family of otters that would live on our dock at night. We'd turn the light on and you'd see them, you know, hanging out, just being otters.'

Taylor spent hours making her own entertainment with other children, making up songs, telling stories and playing games.

She told the *Philadelphia Inquirer*: 'It was really cool living on the bay, and we have so many stories about it. We used to all gather together on the dock when the boat parades would go by on July 4 and we'd shoot water balloons at them. I made a clubhouse in the room above my garage and made a filing system of members of the club. Everyone had a profile that I would write on tiles I found. I painted the whole room different colours and used to spend all day in there just doing nothing but sitting in my little club. Because it was mine. We lived across from the bird sanctuary and I had a pair of binoculars, and some days I'd just stare at the window, looking for birds ... One summer when I was eleven, I wrote a novel. I was allowed to be kind of weird and quirky and imaginative as a kid, and that was my favorite part of living at the Shore.'

The novel, called *Girl Named Girl*, was 350 pages long and based on her friends from home.

'I missed my friends back home so much that I would spend my days locked in the den at the computer just writing a novel,' she explained during a live webcast. 'It included all my friends from school as characters in the novel so I didn't miss them so much, and I would send them back chapters of it.'

Another thing Taylor loved about her holidays was the delicious food – she enjoyed going to eat her favourite white pizzas and giant Caesar salads at the Italian Garden restaurant or indulging in cookies 'n cream ice cream at Springer's store.

She added: 'I remember when I was little, I used to walk in there and just stare up at all the flavours and toppings, completely frozen and unable to make a final decision. I was always so overwhelmed when I went in there.'

Taylor's romantic nature would also make an appearance early when she fell for a boy, who lived next door to their summer home, and began to write one of her first songs, called 'Invisible'.

'I swore I would marry him one day,' she confessed. 'He was the son of my parents' friends. They were always at my house and their son was my age and he would always tell me about the other girls he liked. I felt, well, invisible, obviously.'

Back home, Taylor and her brother went to The Wyndcroft School, a private co-ed school in Pottstown, forty miles from Philadelphia. Both the Swift children were tall, and while Austin excelled at sport, using his height to his advantage, it soon became clear that it wasn't Taylor's strength.

'Everybody thought I'd be good at basketball, but then I tried out and it was like, "Oh." I was awful at anything sports,' she explained to the *Ottawa Citizen*.

However, Taylor did discover what she loved and excelled at: poetry and writing.

While at primary school, she received an assignment to write a two-sentence essay and instead she handed in a two-page composition. Her teacher told Andrea and Scott that there was something different about Taylor that she had never seen before, an innate creative talent.

Her teacher said: 'Even as early as first grade, she was using positional phrases unheard of from kids that age, and by fourth, she was standing out as smart.'

Taylor was mesmerised by the fact that if you put the right number of rhyming words and syllables together, they would sing – or 'bounce' – from the page. When Taylor was ten, she even won a poetry contest with a poem entitled 'Monster in My Closet', which started with the words: 'There's a monster in my closet and I don't know what to do / Have you ever seen him? / Has he ever pounced on you?'

She told the *Washington Post*: 'I picked the most gimmicky one I had to submit. I didn't want to get too dark on them. Poetry was my favorite thing. I loved putting things down on paper. It was so fascinating to me.'

She adored the happy endings in the children's stories she read and the moral messages they conveyed.

'There are a lot of books I loved to read when I was younger that kind of teach you lessons – funny ones like *Amelia Bedelia* or *The Giving Tree*, which teaches you about being kind to others,' she told fans during a webcast. 'Those stories that really have a moral to them are hopefully the first ones that we're presented with by our parents and teachers. If those are the first things you start reading, it can really affect your character. Being good to other people was the main concept I really loved in books.'

Taylor still had no idea that her future lay in music and when asked about what she wanted to do when she grew up, she assumed that she would follow her parents into the heady world of finance.

'I didn't know what a stockbroker was when I was eight, but I would just tell everybody that's what I was going to be,' she recalled. 'We'd be at, like, the first day of school and they're, like, "So what do you guys want to be when you grow up?" And everybody's, like, "I want to be an astronaut!" Or, like, "I want to be a ballerina!" And I'm, like, "I'm gonna be a financial adviser!"'

However, the seeds of her musical career were sown and around this time Taylor started to become interested in musical theatre and got involved in lots of school plays. She loved the rush of getting ready backstage, being under the hot lights and the thunderous applause of the audience. She was determined to shine, even if it meant playing a male role.

She said: 'There was one solo; but it was a guy. It was this character called Freddy Fast Talk and it was the bad guy. I didn't care, I was like, "I will dress up like a guy, I want to sing that song." And so I remember I had, like, a moustache, we drew on eyebrows and we put all my hair up in this hat. So I dressed like a guy and sang the solo.'

In 1999, the Swifts moved to nearby Wyomissing, leaving their farm life behind them. Taylor's new home was a large detached house on a tree-lined avenue in the plush part of the town.

Childhood friend Kaylin Politzer told *Taylor Swift: The Rise of the Nashville Teen*: 'The Swifts' home was beautiful. The stately white house had black shutters with silver moons carved in the sides and was perched on a hill overlooking the city and its surroundings. Taylor had an entire attic to herself – a floor comprised of a games room, painting room and bedroom complete with a canopy bed. I vividly remember Taylor singing along to Nelly Furtado's "I'm Like a Bird" as I watched from that canopy bed.'

The Swift children enrolled at West Reading Elementary School. While it was only a few miles from her last school, it was a completely different world and Taylor struggled to fit in.

'I didn't have friends,' she told the *Reading Eagle*. 'No one talked to me . . . I didn't know anybody.'

The school straddled two areas: one had high crime rates and extreme poverty; and the other was where wealthy business owners settled with their families in larger, more palatial homes. Taylor's unpopularity was because many of her new classmates were jealous of her comfortable home life.

Another girl added: 'Taylor found it hard to make friends. People used to call her stuck up. I guess they were jealous. She wanted for nothing, when some of them couldn't scrape a few cents together. She was daddy's little princess and had parents who adored her, whereas some of the other kids were from broken homes. One girl I knew would do fake retching when Taylor walked by. She felt Taylor's parents were unconditionally supportive of her and that made her nauseous. Taylor also got good grades and had a perfect home life so she was an easy target for jealousy.'

Despite the difficult start, Taylor excelled in lessons, especially in drama and singing. Her teachers, like those at her previous school, quickly became aware of Taylor's talents and suggested to Andrea that they find another outlet for her, so she enrolled in the local children's theatre company, Berks Youth Theatre Academy. She started out in the chorus for the show *Annie* as one of the scruffy orphans, but was quickly cast into the impressive lead roles, such as Sandy in *Grease*, Maria in *The Sound of Music* and Conrad in *Bye Bye Birdie*. Through this she connected with other like-minded peers.

Even though this was traditional musical theatre, Taylor sang with a country twang to her voice.

'I was playing the role of Sandy in *Grease* and it just came out sounding country,' she said to GAC. 'It was all I had listened to, so I guess it was just kind of natural.'

She also had singing and acting lessons in her spare time. Her first voice teacher was a man named Kirk Cremer, who spotted her potential and worked tirelessly with her to develop her young voice. She became part of his TheatreKids Live! group and Kirk noted that, even at this tender age, Taylor had natural comedic talent.

Her ambition and tenacity were growing by the day; she ignored her jealous peers and dreamed of treading the boards, even going to a number of auditions for glitzy Broadway and off-Broadway plays in nearby New York. Kirk became her first manager, arranging for headshots to be photographed and accompanying her to auditions.

'When I was growing up in Pennsylvania, auditioning for Broadway was my dream,' she explained to *Inquirer Entertainment*. 'I went to several auditions in New York. I was always going there for vocal and acting lessons ... and for auditions, where we would stand in line in a long hallway with a lot of people ... I never lost my passion for theatre.'

However, as much as she loved musicals and even though she had started listening to more mainstream pop music like the Spice Girls, Natasha Bedingfield and Hanson to fit in with her classmates, Taylor was still passionate about country music and artists such as Shania Twain, Faith Hill and the Dixie Chicks.

'My interest [in musical theatre] soon drew me to country music,' she told the *Reading Eagle*. 'I was infatuated with the sound, with the storytelling. I could relate to it. I can't really tell you why. With me it's instinctual.' She continued: 'Ever since I discovered their music I wanted to do country music. I wanted to sing country music. Didn't matter if I lived in Pennsylvania. Didn't matter if everybody at my school was like, "You-you? Play country music? Why do you like country music? You're so weird."'

She said Shania Twain, who is sometimes referred to as the Queen of Country Pop because her music reaches a broader audience, had the biggest influence on her.

'She came out, and she was just so strong and so independent and wrote all her own songs,' she told *Time* magazine. 'That meant so much to me, even as a 10-year-old. Just knowing that the stories she was telling in those songs – those were her stories.'

After theatre-company shows, they would have a party to celebrate. This was Taylor's favourite part of the whole event: she would take to the stage, grab the microphone and belt out some country classics.

'The thing that I really looked forward to most was at the cast party after the shows they would have karaoke machines set up and that was when I could sing country music,' she said.

It was Kirk Cremer's mother Sandy Wielder who suggested that Taylor seemed more natural to pursue a career in country music rather than theatre and Taylor welcomed the idea. She started performing at local fairs, with ever-increasing audiences.

As soon as she got a taste of singing country in front of other people there was no stopping her and she regularly sang karaoke in a smoky bar about half an hour away. Owned by a man called Pat Garrett, who had several big country hits in the 1980s, the bar held open-mic competitions for aspiring singers.

'I started singing karaoke in his roadhouse – his little bar – when I was ten years old,' she told CMT news. 'He'll vouch that I was there every single week saying, "I'm just going to come back if you don't let me win one." I was kind of like an annoying flag around the place. I would not leave them alone. What they would do is have these karaoke contests . . . I would go until I won.'

Taylor, who explained her parents were 'kind of embarrassed by it', played every week without fail for two whole years and Pat was so impressed by her stamina that he arranged for her to be the opening act for the Charlie Daniels Band, another popular country act. Bizarrely, her booking was at 10.30 a.m. before his 8.30 p.m. show and the audience was sparse. However, he also organised for her to perform at the Bloomsburg Fair, a huge outdoor event, where she sang a couple of tracks with a backing band in front of hundreds of spectators. At first, she was understandably nervous but she soon started to enjoy herself.

'It was a little scary at first . . . Once, somebody told me to picture the audience in their underpants,' she told CMT.com, laughing. 'That does not work at all.'

She later explained to *Elle Girl* that the more she sang in front of big audiences, the easier, and more exciting, it became.

'Every time you play another show, it gets better and better . . . Anything you start doing is going to be scary.'

It was like a drug to her and Taylor would not stop dreaming of where her performances might lead. She soon earned a reputation as being a 'small girl with a big voice' and when she was eleven, she sang the US national anthem to an audience of thousands at a match for the famous basketball team, the Philadelphia 76ers. The huge rap star Jay-Z was in the audience and gave her a high five when she finished. She couldn't believe that such a massive star had thought she had done a good job. She was ecstatic.

Taylor was no ordinary kid and Kirk knew that – he could see that she had something special about her and an innate musical ability, so he organised for her to record her own demo album with his older brother, Ronnie, who owned a studio. As she sang into the mic with her headphones on, Taylor felt like LeAnn Rimes and even recorded her track 'One Way Ticket', along with 'Here You Come Again' by Dolly Parton, 'There's Your Trouble' by the Dixie Chicks and a version of 'Hopelessly Devoted to You' from *Grease*.

Taylor's obsession with country music continued; from the storytelling and catchy lyrics, to the Southern twangs and cowboy fashions, she was fixated. One day, she watched a TV programme, *Behind the Music*, on the VH1 channel, about the huge country singer Faith Hill, which said that she had been discovered in Nashville. It was like an epiphany. From that moment onwards, Taylor became obsessive about going there. Home to the famous Music Row and venues like the Grand Ole Opry, Ryman Auditorium, Country Music Hall of Fame and the Wildhorse Saloon, Nashville was the very heartbeat of the country-music world.

'Of course I got it in my head that there was this magical land called Nashville where dreams come true and that's where I needed to go,' she recalled to the *Daily Telegraph*. 'I began absolutely non-stop tormenting my parents, begging them on a daily basis to move there.'

Her parents – who she described as 'pie-in-the-sky Dad, down-to-earth Mom' – were blown away by their daughter's talents and were always supportive and encouraged her.

Taylor recalled to the *Independent*: 'As I grew up, [my mom] would always say to me, "You can do whatever you want in life – as long as you work hard to get there. You have to work hard for every single baby step that you take that is closer to what you want – and we will support that until you change your mind and do something else. And when you want to do something else, we will be your cheerleaders in that too."'

Taylor perhaps had Andrea to thank for her tenacity and resolve. As Taylor's childhood friend Kaylin Politzer mused: 'I remember being both in constant awe and fear of Taylor's mother. I remember her being loving and encouraging but she was also a no-nonsense woman with a fiery spirit and quick tongue . . . To this day, I don't know if I've ever met a more tenacious lady. She didn't need a stage to command attention.'

Taylor had clearly inherited her determination, which would not waver; she wanted to be a music star and nothing would stand in her way.

During the holidays when Taylor was eleven, Andrea caved in to her daughter's desire to go to Nashville together with Austin – they travelled 650 miles to get there.

As Taylor gazed up the famous Music Row, home to all the big record labels, housed in vast buildings, she was in her element. She had finally made it to the fairy-tale world of Music City, where she thought her wishes would be granted.

Andrea told her daughter that now she had brought her, it would be Taylor who put in the legwork.

'I made it really clear,' Andrea told *Teen Superstar*. 'Okay, if this is something you want, you've got to do it . . . I'm not a stage mom. I didn't sign up to dive her into the music business, so I would walk to the front door and wait for her. She went to every place on Music Row.'

As her mum drove down the famous street, Taylor would

shout out the names of the huge labels, hop out of the car and then bravely knock on some of country music's most important doors with her demo CD in hand. It had a black-and-white cover and a picture of her with the words, CALL ME. On the back it had her email address and telephone number.

She explained: 'My mom would stop outside a record label and I would run in and hand my CD to the reception-ist and would be like, "Hi, I'm Taylor, I'm 11 and I want a record deal, call me."'

The receptionists were used to a constant flood of wannabes looking for their moment in the spotlight and unlike in the more cut-throat world of Los Angeles and New York, they were kind and welcoming. Taylor was bursting with excitement and nerves about who might listen to her voice and, when they returned home, she waited on tenter-hooks for the phone to ring.

'I was like, "If I want to sing music, I'm going to need a record deal,"' she summed up. 'So, I'm going to get a record deal. I really thought it was easy.'

In the end, only one person replied to say thank you for her CD and told her to keep trying. Naturally, she was disappointed, but rather than putting her off, the trip made her more resolute than ever to succeed. She took away a valuable lesson: now she knew there were hundreds of girls flocking to Nashville every day to try to break into the music world and she had to stand out to give herself an edge over the other new talent looking for a deal.

'I didn't realize that there were hundreds of people in

Nashville trying to do exactly what I was trying to do, and that everybody had the same dream,' she said. 'I thought, "You don't just make it in Nashville. I've really got to work on something that would make me different."'

Taylor was in luck. She had a 12-string guitar but she had struggled to learn to play it because her fingers were too small, so the instrument was just sitting in the corner gathering dust. One day, shortly after her trip to Nashville, a computer repairman came over to her house; he saw the guitar, picked it up and started to play. It was the push that she needed. The repairman taught Taylor just three basic chords – A, D and E – and on the same day, she composed her first song.

Speaking to *CMT Insider*, she said: 'I went home and decided I needed to learn a few more things before I went back. I learned guitar and I learned songwriting, and I never put it down.'

Eight minutes long, her first song was entitled 'Lucky You'. It was about a girl who dares to be different.

She said during a webcast: 'It somehow got leaked online and it is a terrifying experience when people bring it up because I'm like, "I sound like a chipmunk." But you look back on your first experiences with writing and every one of those experiences turns you into who you're going to be.'

Even after a teacher at school continued to tell her that her hands were too small for the 12-string, Taylor persisted. She spent up to four hours a day trying to master the instrument. She got calluses on her fingers, which would crack and bleed because of her dogged perseverance. Rather than stop when her fingers hurt, she would just tape them up and carry on.

She said: 'At first, it seemed really hard and then I realised that if I put my mind to something that it was really mind over matter and maybe my fingers weren't long enough or developed enough to play it but I played it. It's really exciting to see that. I'm like, "Ha, guitar teacher!"'

She started lessons with Ronnie Cremer and the first proper song she learned was the Dixie Chicks' 'Cowboy Take Me Away'. She then started composing her own songs during every spare second she had, even while at school.

She said: 'I would find time to write either in class and when the teachers would conduct random notebook checks, you can imagine their surprise when it is algebra on one side of the page and songs on the other side . . .'

One of her earliest songs was inspired by watching LeAnn Rimes in concert and called 'Kid in the Crowd'. The message behind the song was that for every performer on stage, there was a fan watching them who wanted to make it big. Taylor was that girl; she was determined to be a huge star, no matter what.

CHAPTER TWO

'I was writing from pain'

While she loved her music, Taylor's new fascination with country music and songwriting meant that she was starting to become more isolated from her school friends at Wyomissing Area Junior High School, who described her as 'annoying'. Like most youngsters, no one liked the kooky girl who was different from them.

'The kids at school would make fun of me,' she told *Vogue*. 'They didn't think I was cool or pretty enough, so they stopped talking to me.'

The bullies whispered about her in the corridors, avoided sitting with her at lunchtime and made up jokes at her expense. Taylor was an outcast.

Songwriting became her sanctuary and she admitted that she couldn't wait to get home every night to write more tracks. Being shunned by her peers allowed her to observe them and write about her feelings.

'I first started writing songs because I didn't really have anyone else to talk to,' she told *InStyle* magazine. 'As sad as that sounds, I was going through this really hard time at school where I didn't have any friends. Songwriting for me just started out as therapy.' She added: 'When you're dealing with something like loneliness or confusion or rejection or frustration, those emotions are so jumbled up in your head.'

All the kids were on the verge of becoming teenagers but while her classmates started to become interested in going to parties and dating boys, Taylor just wanted to stay in her room and play her guitar. She would never cave in to peer pressure and her desire to be a singer would not wane.

Taylor said all the popular girls started going out, breaking into their parents' drinks cabinets and flirting with boys. She felt she had the choice of either being friends with them and 'messing her life up', or being a loner.

Recalling an incident when she was twelve, she told the *New Yorker*: 'At the beginning of the year, we were all sleeping over at somebody's house and they were all talking about how they wanted to sneak over to this guy's house because this guy had beer. And I was just, like . . . "I want to call my mom! I want to call my mom! I want to call my mom!" My whole life I've never felt comfortable just being . . . edgy like that.'

She also told the *Daily Mail*: 'I was considered weird because I would play singer-songwriter nights instead of going to parties. I think it's weird to go to parties and get drunk when you're, like, twelve – but whatever!'

Even though she was yet to have a boyfriend, or even be kissed, Taylor would watch the kids in her class as they started going out on dates and write about it. In her lyrics she assumed the persona of someone far more experienced.

'I found that I was alone a lot of the time, kind of on the outside looking into their discussions, and the things they were saying to each other,' she said to CMT.com. 'I started developing this really keen sense of observation – of how to watch people and see what they did. From that sense I was able to write songs about relationships when I was thirteen but not in relationships.'

Every day was a big ordeal for the budding songstress, especially at lunchtime when she would sit down at the communal table to eat and the other girls who were sitting there would raise their eyebrows, laugh and then get up and move somewhere else.

She told *E! True Hollywood Story*: 'I would literally walk up and sit down at the lunch table full of girls and they would all get up and leave as soon as I sat down. I could take what happened that day and turn it into something good. I could write songs and that's where I could be happy.'

It wasn't just her love of music that marked Taylor out as different. At 5 feet 11 inches tall, she felt gangly and out of place with her pale skin and unruly hair.

She told *BOP*: 'At school, I hated having curly hair because all the cool, popular girls had straight hair. I would try to straighten my hair, but it didn't really straighten that well! It would always have lumps in it, and in the back I'd leave one piece curly by accident.'

When she was twelve, Taylor wrote a song called 'The Outside', about being an outcast and not fitting in, and another, 'My Turn to Be Me', a track about not feeling like you have to fit in. Her words had sincerity and conviction.

'I was writing from pain,' she said to *Entertainment Weekly*. 'I've always felt so lucky because I've never needed an escape in drink and drugs – music has always been that escape for me.'

There was one particularly painful memory that stands out for Taylor: when she asked a group of girls to go shopping to the local mall with her and they all said they were busy. In the end, she decided to go with her mum and when they arrived they saw her so-called friends, who were all together, laughing and having fun. Taylor was tearful and heartbroken but instead of dwelling on it, she and her mum drove an hour and a half away to an even better shopping centre.

Taylor recalled: 'That memory is one of those painful ones you'll never fully get over. At that point I'd been shunned from the group for whatever reason and I was still desperately trying to be included . . . In situations like that, my mum has always known exactly the right time to run away. There are situations where you have to encourage someone to be tough, then there are times when you should just run . . . We showed them in our own little way. We had a great time.'

That evening she wrote a song called 'The Best Day', which featured on her second album, *Fearless*. Taylor later recorded it in secret and synched it up with home videos and gave it to her mum one Christmas. Andrea, who remains her closest ally, burst into floods of tears when she watched it and says that the song still brings tears to her eyes every time she hears it.

Understandably, Andrea found it very hard watching her daughter being so introverted and listening to the heartfelt lyrics she was producing in her bedroom.

'My worst time of the day was going to pick Taylor up from school,' she recalled. 'Because I'd have to hear about the ostracizing.' She explained to the *Daily Mail*: 'As a parent, there's no bigger pain than watching your child being rejected by her peers. But it made me realise, if she was ready to sacrifice being accepted and having friends for the lonely experience of writing songs in her bedroom then it must mean a lot to her.'

And unlike most teenage girls and their mums, Taylor and Andrea never fell out.

'My mom has never been condescending,' Taylor told website The Boot. 'She's not the kind of person that needs to be perfect all the time and needs me to see no flaws in her. The coolest thing about my mom is she's always been so real with me, and honest no matter what ... Even when I was a pre-teen that's when I needed her the most. That's usually when people are [at the] too-cool-for-their-parents stage. Well, I was really not cool enough for anyone but my parents at that phase. I had no friends! My mom was the one person that I could turn to and who never, ever, hurt me.'

Taylor explained that Andrea would rally her spirits by taking her on day trips to try to take her mind off her problems at school.

'She would just take me on these adventures and we

would drive around and go to towns we'd never seen before,' she said to Taste of Country website. 'Those adventures and those days of just running away from my problems – you're not supposed to run away from problems, but when you're thirteen and your friends won't talk to you and your mom lets you run from those problems, I think it's a good thing ... My mom was my escape in a lot of ways.'

The bullying didn't dampen her fierce ambition and Taylor was never one to wait for opportunities to come to her. Instead, she tried to create them for herself, taking every chance she could and singing in front of every audience she could find, even when they were on holiday in New Jersey.

Talking to *CMT Insider*, she said: 'Instead of playing at karaoke bars and things like that where I needed to drag my little karaoke machine everywhere, I would go with my guitar and plug it in at coffee houses, and I would bring my little amplifier and plug it in at Boy Scout meetings. I would plug it in at all these different places, little random places where you could go and play. I now had a portable instrument, and I could go accompany myself, and I could play anywhere I wanted to. That really expanded the places where I could play and my abilities. I played so much that I came a long way in a short period of time.'

Her drive was fired by fear she might not live out her dream. Taylor knew she had something special.

She later explained to *Cosmo Girl*: 'I was so driven because I didn't expect that anything would just happen for me. That doubt fuelled me to work harder. My attitude was the opposite of most people who are like, "It's gonna happen for me, it's gonna happen for me." My mantra was always, "It's not gonna happen for me. Go out and play a show or it's not gonna happen."'

When she was thirteen, she was asked to sing the US national anthem again, this time at the US Open tennis championship in New York, and she jumped at the chance.

'It occurred to me that the national anthem was the best way to get in front of a large group of people if you don't have a record deal,' she told *Rolling Stone*. 'So I started singing the national anthem everywhere I possibly could . . . I would sing it at garden-club meetings. I didn't care. I figured out that if you could sing that one song, you could get in front of 20,000 people without even having a record deal. So I sang that song many, many, many, many times.'

Taylor's plan paid off and she caught the eye of New York-based music manager Dan Dymtrow, who has represented artists such as Britney Spears. He requested more information about her and her father sent him a home video.

'My dad put together this typical "dad video" type of thing with the cat chewing the neck [of my guitar] and stuff like that,' she recalled to *Wood & Steel*. 'Dan called and asked us to come down and play for him in his office, so I brought my first 12-string down and played some songs for him.'

Dan immediately signed her up and quickly got to work promoting her. With his help, Taylor modelled for Abercrombie & Fitch as part of their 'Rising Stars' campaign in *Vanity Fair*, which was a very popular one with high-school kids.

'Dan sent the company a press kit and they immediately called him back and were like, "Yeah, we want her on the shoot,"' Taylor relayed to the *Nashville City Paper*. 'I was just thinking, "I'm not cool enough for this, it's Abercrombie & Fitch!"'

Taylor appeared in denim jeans and a white top, with her guitar slung over her shoulder, wiping a tear from her eye.

She also had an original song included in the Maybelline cosmetics compilation CD called *Chicks with Attitude* and she featured in a programme entitled 'Nashville Dreams' for *Good Morning America*.

However, as her fame rose and her fledgling career started to take shape, the bullying at school increased, much to Taylor's dismay. Tellingly, one classmate admitted to *Taylor Swift: The Rise of the Nashville Teen* that they were jealous.

'We treated Taylor like crap, but you know why? We were absolutely downright jealous,' she revealed. 'Her star shone so brightly, it eclipsed the rest of us and made us feel inferior. Excluding her was one way we could get our power back. We didn't necessarily all want to sing, but a lot of us liked the idea of being famous and I know we at least all wanted to feel special. Taylor took that away from us. She was always the topic of conversation.'

Taylor ignored them and focussed on her commitment. Dan Dymtrow regularly took her to meetings with major record labels in Nashville and their persistence paid off: she was starting to get noticed more and more for her sugar-coated charm, superb songwriting skills and her perfect poise.

RCA Records, home to stars such as Christina Aguilera, Kelly Clarkson and Dave Matthews, were the first to act and offered her a 'development deal'.

'I played them a few songs and they said they wanted to sign me to a development deal,' Taylor explained on *Teen Superstar*. 'A development deal is an in-between record deal. It's like a guy saying that he wants to date you but not be your boyfriend. They don't want to sign you to an actual record deal and put an album out on you. They want to watch your progress for a year.'

When Dan broke the news, she was over the moon and grinning from ear to ear. She knew it could be the start of something huge for her, although nothing was guaranteed.

'It's a non-committal commitment,' she said to *CMT Insider*, 'but I was elated. I was just, "Oh, my gosh! This huge record label wants to sign me to a development deal. I'm so excited!"'

The label gave her recording time and sponsorship money, but there was no promise of an album at the end of it. Nonetheless, the Swifts bowed to their daughter's ambition and moved: they also believed their daughter could make it. They had witnessed first hand the lengths to which she was prepared to go to reach her goals.

'My father had a job he could do from anywhere,' Taylor told *Blender* magazine. 'My parents moved across the country so I could pursue a dream.'

Taylor's dad, Scott, who she described as a 'big teddy bear who tells me everything I do is perfect' sought advice from Pat Garrett about the music business. Pat, who was an industry veteran, admitted he was bowled over by Taylor's ambition.

He told CBS News: 'Her dad showed me a notebook she had, and in this ring notebook the only thing she had was her signature, practising her autograph. She has an insatiable drive.'

Her father arranged a transfer to the Nashville office of Merrill Lynch and the Swifts bought a large house overlooking a peaceful lake, around half an hour from the centre in Hendersonville, Tennessee, a family-friendly town. The house was on the same road, called Old Hickory Lane, where other big stars lived, including Roy Orbison and the late Johnny Cash. It was a quiet and peaceful countryside setting but was near enough to get to Nashville for Taylor's work.

Scott, who is a keen sailor, told Searay website: 'When Andrea found the place on Old Hickory Lane, we stopped at the dock on the way to check up on the house. I looked down the cove toward the lake, imagined my Sea Ray [boat] tied up there and said, "I'll take it." She said, "Don't you want to see the house first?"'

Scott went on to found an investment banking and financial advisory company called the Swift Group.

Taylor later said she realised what a sacrifice her parents had made by moving but Andrea and Scott were sensitive to her feelings.

Andrea told *Entertainment Weekly*'s ew.com: 'I never wanted to make that move about her "making it." Because what a horrible thing if it hadn't happened, for her to carry that kind of guilt or pressure around. And we moved far enough outside Nashville to where she didn't have to be going to school with producers' kids and label presidents' kids and be reminded constantly that she was struggling to make it. We've always told her that this is not about putting food on our table or making our dreams come true. There would always be an escape hatch into normal life if she decided this wasn't something she had to pursue. And of course that's like saying to her, "If you want to stop breathing, that's cool."'

Taylor and Austin enrolled in the local school, Hendersonville High School. They settled quickly and Taylor's classmates were much friendlier towards her. Most of them had grown up around country music and were impressed by her talent.

Taylor told the *New Yorker*: 'Everybody was so nice to me! They're all, like, "We heard you're a singer. We have a talent show next week – do you want to enter?"'

On her first day, she met her best friend, a girl called Abigail Anderson, who became one of Taylor's biggest fans.

'First day of school we sat next to each other in English,' Taylor told Oprah Winfrey. 'She wanted to be a swimmer and go off on a school scholarship for swimming and I wanted to be a singer.'

The girls would mess around together in silly voices, giggling at their inside jokes and generally having fun.

'[Abigail and I] kind of came to the conclusion in ninth grade that we were never going to be popular,' she told the *Los Angeles Times*, 'so we should just stick together and have fun and not take ourselves too seriously.' The girls kept each other grounded and Abigail would also inspire one of Taylor's huge hits, 'Fifteen', about what they went through at that time.

One of the classes Taylor loved was English, where she devoured the classics, including Harper Lee's *To Kill a Mockingbird*, which she said 'really changed the way I looked at life'.

Taylor had felt awkward and out of place at her old school but she had finally put those dark days behind her and she had a large group of friends who thought she was great. Many of those friends were boys but Taylor admitted that she was never a 'boy magnet'.

'There was always the girl all the guys liked and wanted to date, but it was never me,' she confessed to the *Daily Mail*. 'It would have been fun to find out what that would have been like, though. I've always been a girl's girl.'

However, soon she was attracting boys and going on dates. She was fifteen when she had her first kiss – much later than most of her peers – and after her first boyfriend played a big part in shaping her style: she started to embrace her blonde curls and dressed-down fashions. She finally felt comfortable in her own skin, with her natural curls, minimal make-up and porcelain-pale skin.

She said: 'My first boyfriend would make subtle suggestions like, "I like your hair straight – you should do that more often." So I'd straighten it all the time. Or he'd say, "You look good with a tan," so I was tanning every day. It hit me that I didn't want to be the version of myself that he approved of, so I had to end it.'

One of her first boyfriends was a guy named Brandon Borello, who inspired the track, 'Our Song'. Taylor and Brandon didn't have 'a song' and when Taylor needed a track to perform at the school talent show, she decided she would compose one for them.

She told music.aol.com: 'I wrote this song in my freshman year of high school for my ninth-grade talent show. I was sitting there thinking, "I've gotta write an upbeat song that's gonna relate to everyone." And at that time I was dating a guy and we didn't have a song. So I wrote us one, and I played it at the show. Months later, people would come up to me and say, "I loved that song you played." They'd only heard it once so I thought, "There must be something here."'

Taylor continued to write new tracks in every spare moment – scribbling on anything she could get her hands on, from Kleenex to schoolbooks. Sometimes, she even rushed into the toilet in the middle of class, to hum a new melody and record it on her mobile phone. It was as if she dreamed in music and lyrics. Everything she saw, touched, heard, became inspiration for her music and her friends and family were behind her one hundred per cent.

'They were so supportive,' she explained. 'I hung out with them as much as possible.'

Taylor would often test out her new songs on her bunch of friends – as she said, they were exactly the audience she was trying to attract. Many evenings they would sit around the campfire in the balmy evening sun listening to Taylor strumming on her guitar and singing her latest melody.

One of her guy friends at the time, she said, was someone she had feelings for who didn't realise and she composed a song about it called 'I Lie'. Everything that happened around Taylor informed her songs.

'You can draw inspiration from anything,' she told the *Washington Post*. 'If you're a good storyteller, you can take a dirty look somebody gives you or a guy you used to have flirtations with starts dating a new girl, or somebody you're casually talking to says something that makes you so mad – you can create an entire scenario around that. You don't have to date people or be married to people to write songs about them.'

With her RCA job, Taylor had writing sessions with Music City's biggest names. Most country writers would compose with others; it was very rare to see just one name on a song-writing credit and new writers would often work with one or even two others, so co-writing was the norm. After school, Andrea would pick Taylor up and ferry her to the studios, where she would sit down with different composers.

Taylor told *American Songwriter* magazine: 'I knew that going into those meetings with those hit songwriters was something I was lucky to get to do. And I knew that being a 14-year-old girl, anybody would – understandably – think, "I'm gonna have to write a song for a kid today". But I didn't want anyone to walk out of the meeting thinking, "I wrote a song for a kid today." So, I would walk in with ten or fifteen almost-finished songs. Or with developed ideas – finished melodies or choruses. I just wanted to make sure that everybody knew I was serious about it. That I didn't just take it lightly."

She wanted to be taken seriously and once declared during a press conference: 'I didn't come into this to be babysat.'

Her ability to write passionate songs had been noted elsewhere in Nashville. Sony / ATV publishing house could see her incredible aptitude for songwriting and gave her a contract to write tracks for their artists, making her their youngest contracted songwriter.

Taylor was thrilled but she knew she faced an uphill battle to be taken seriously by the country-music circuit. She was a teenager very much in an adult world and many were sceptical about her talents.

'When I signed I knew I had to work just as hard as the veteran 45-year-old writers who were also signed there,' she explained to *Songwriter Universe*.

She impressed her co-writers from the start and Sony / ATV president Troy Tomlinson told MusicRadar website: 'She's among the very few artists who are born with a gift that just rolls out of her. I still marvel at how this young girl with limited life experiences at that point could write such lyrics and melodies. She was born with it, that gift.'

Taylor made a key relationship at this time with another writer called Liz Rose, who would prove instrumental to her career. After Liz saw her play at a songwriting event and suggested they try working together, the pair began collaborating for two hours every Tuesday afternoon. They would start by nibbling on Hershey's Kisses chocolates so Taylor 'could get her energy up' and then they would start composing. Liz, who was in her forties at the time, admitted that at first she was doubtful about working with someone so young but in the end they really gelled.

'I think she ended up just writing with me because I didn't change what she was doing,' Liz told *American Songwriter*. 'I tried to make it better and mould it and hone it, and hang on there and write it down; that's why it worked with us. I really respected her and got what she was trying to do and I didn't want to make her write in the Nashville cookie-cutter songwriting mould.'

Taylor's greatest source of material was from school: the boys she dated and knew; her classmates and their short-lived relationships; and the pressures and worries of being a normal teenager.

Talking to US music magazine *Blender*, Liz said: 'Basically, I was just her editor. She'd write about what happened in school that day. She had such a clear vision of what she was trying to say. And she'd come in with the most incredible hooks.'

One of the songs Taylor and Liz composed at this time was a bittersweet track called 'Tim McGraw'.

Liz said: 'I remember her coming in and saying, "I wanna write a song called 'When You Think Tim McGraw,'" and the first thing that went through my mind was, "Okay, we're gonna write this song, and you don't have a record deal, and nobody else is gonna cut it." I said, "Okay! I'm not gonna argue!"'

Knowing that she and her boyfriend Brandon would

break up because he was going to college, Taylor thought of all the things that he might think about while he was away and the first thing that came into her mind was the music of US country star Tim McGraw. McGraw was a massive star. He and his wife Faith Hill were considered the King and Queen of the Country World and his previous eight albums had all debuted at No. 1 on the *Billboard* Country Albums chart. Taylor loved his music and said that during a maths class she just started humming the melody; becoming upset thinking about Brandon's imminent departure, she did what she knew best and wrote about it. The single captured the sweetness and sadness of first love.

'It was reminiscent, and it was thinking about a relationship you had and then lost,' she told *Entertainment Weekly*. 'I think one of the most powerful human emotions is what should have been and wasn't . . . That was a really good song to start out on, just because a lot of people can relate to wanting what you can't have.'

With her creative juices flowing, she penned another track, the tender ballad 'Teardrops on My Guitar'. After she had got over Brandon's departure, Taylor fell for a good-looking guy called Drew Hardwick, but even though they were good friends, he had no idea how she felt about him.

Taylor recalled to *Country Standard Time*: 'I used to have a huge crush on this guy, Drew, who would sit there every day talking to me about another girl: how beautiful she was, how nice, and how smart and perfect she was. I sat there and listened and said, "Oh I'm so happy for you." I guess this is a good example of how I let my feelings out in songs and sometimes no other way. I love this song because of its honesty and vulnerability. To this day, Drew and his girlfriend are still together."

One of her tracks, a rocky and angry hit, was called 'Picture to Burn' and was inspired by a cocky guy who Taylor almost dated but didn't.

She told GAC: 'I found myself just sitting there with my guitar, going, "I hate this stupid truck that he doesn't let me drive, he's such a redneck! Oh, my God!" That actually became the chorus to the song, so that's one of the most honest songs I've written.'

She also said it had a funny side to it and she thought other girls would connect with it.

'I think girls can relate to the song because basically it's about just being mad,' she explained. 'And it's okay to be mad after a breakup or after something goes wrong with a relationship. It's just like completely, brutally honest. It's also kind of funny. It's got a comedic edge to it.'

After Taylor and Liz finished a song, they needed it recorded to a good quality and they started collaborating with a young producer called Nathan Chapman, who was also trying to get his foot in the door of the multi-million-dollar country scene. Nathan, who worked out of a 'shack' behind the Sony office, was willing to try new things and wanted to bring a fresh sound to his work. He became the perfect colleague and really understood Taylor's vision.

He told *Chattanooga Times Free Press*: 'My role as a producer is to help get her ideas out. She may have a particular kind of guitar in mind; she'll describe it to me and I'll help her realise that.'

While her writing was going well with Sony, there was devastating news from RCA and her development deal: they decided to pass on her. They wanted to keep her in development until she was eighteen and for her to record music composed by other writers. They simply weren't sold on her work. Taylor was absolutely gutted; she felt ready to launch her career performing her own material.

'Basically, there were three things that were going to happen,' Taylor explained to the *Daily Telegraph*. 'They were going to drop me, shelve me – that's kind of like putting me in cold storage – or give me a record deal. The only one of those you want is a record deal.'

Taylor didn't want to be put 'on hold' and made a huge, life-changing decision: she walked away from the biggest record company in Nashville. It was 2005 and she was still just fourteen years old.

Talking to *Entertainment Weekly*, she said: 'We just decided that we wanted to look around, so we walked. And it's not a really popular thing to do in Nashville, to walk away from a major record deal. But that's what I did, because I wanted to find some place that would really put a lot of time and care into this.'

Taylor was unfaltering in her vision. She wanted to write and perform her own material and work with a record label that would help her develop her talents on her own terms. She felt like her work was ready to be recorded and released there and then. She couldn't relate to other people's work in the same way she understood and felt her own distinctive songs in her heart. She knew that by singing other people's material, it wouldn't give her the chance to be unique.

'I didn't want to just be another girl singer,' she explained. 'I wanted there to be something that set me apart. And I knew that had to be my writing. Also, it was a big, big record label with big superstars, and I felt like I needed my own direction and the kind of attention that a little label will give you. I just did not want it to happen with the method of, "Let's throw this up against the wall and see if it sticks, and if it doesn't, we'll just walk away." I wanted a record label that needed me, that absolutely was counting on me to succeed. I love that pressure.'

She explained to GAC that for her, it was very much a black-and-white choice. Taylor showed not only maturity but courage and fearlessness in making this massive decision.

'Basically, there are two types of people – people who see me as an artist and judge me by my music. The other people judge me by a number – my age, which means nothing.'

She got straight back to work and continued writing for Sony but kept taking her demos to different record-label executives. It was relentless but Taylor felt that if she worked hard enough it would pay off.

She was definitely on everyone's radar but they were all waiting for her to mature. Many stars in the country-music business had made it young, including LeAnn Rimes and Dolly Parton, but most had failed and their music careers had sunk before they had even begun.

'I can understand,' Taylor remarked to CMT.com. 'They were afraid to put out a 13-year-old. They were afraid to put out a 14-year-old. They were afraid to put out a 15-year-old. Then they were nervous about putting out a 16-year-old.'

She also parted ways with Dan Dymtrow, who later filed a lawsuit against her. It was a challenging time but Taylor faced it head-on with her normal charisma. While she had a blissful home life she had struggled in the past and she drew on her inner strength, looking at the new phase in her career with her typical cup-half-full outlook.

'Being able to face the rejections in Nashville is nothing compared to facing the rejections in middle school,' she joked to the *Miami Herald*.

One man in particular saw Taylor's potential: one of the youngest and brightest young record executives in Nashville at the time, Scott Borchetta, was working at Universal Records. The first song of Taylor's he ever heard was a demo recording of 'Teardrops on My Guitar' and he was impressed.

Taylor's next move was to set up a showcase for herself at the Bluebird Café, a legendary venue, where many country stars have gone to perform and launch their careers. It is a venue that takes its musicians and songwriters very seriously, with a no-talking rule when performers take to the small stage.

It was 4 November 2004, a month before her fifteenth birthday. Taylor invited everyone she knew, from music executives to publishers and publicists. She might have been a seasoned singer, but her heart was pounding and she was petrified. She knew that this was the most important performance to date.

Everyone who was invited came, including Scott Borchetta, and they crammed into the small venue as Taylor took to the stage with her trusty guitar, dressed in blue denim, a pretty top and with her curly hair cascading down her back. She adjusted the microphone, introduced herself and started singing.

Andrea said she looked over and noticed the look of awe on Scott Borchetta's face as he watched the young singer pour her heart and soul into her music.

'I looked across the room and I saw this person just watching her play, absolutely immersed in her music. I thought to myself, "I don't know who that is but I hope that's the guy who ends up working with her."'

Speaking about the showcase during a TV interview with *CBS This Morning*, Scott added: 'What I saw in Taylor was . . . just a great artist. Even at fourteen years old I was enamoured by her songwriting prowess, and just her prowess. So I just always saw her as a great artist.'

Scott quickly tried to contact her and, after leaving a series of voicemails, finally managed to get hold of her but cryptically told her they couldn't speak on the phone.

Taylor told GAC: 'He was like, "I'm going to be doing something and I need to talk to you in person but I don't trust the phone." And I was like, "If you don't trust the phone, there has got to be something going on that I don't know about."'

Eventually, they met in his office late one evening, when

his colleagues had gone for the day, so they would have some privacy.

Scott had been growing restless in his job and told Taylor and her family that he had both good news and bad news: the good news was that he loved her and wanted to sign her but the bad news was that he was leaving Universal Records. He offered to introduce her to his fellow Universal executives but said he would be leaving before long and they wouldn't work together. He promised her that if she waited, he would do his best to make her a success on his own record label and that he understood her vision and he wanted her to record her own music.

'There is nobody like her out there,' Scott told GAC. 'She has a great attitude. She is a hard worker. She is a teenager . . . I was smitten. I couldn't get up in the morning and not have her on my record label.'

It was a tough world with only a small fraction of new companies succeeding but there was instant chemistry. Just like Taylor, Scott Borchetta was bold, cool and willing to take risks.

'You can tell when someone really gets you,' Taylor said. 'The best part of getting a record deal was it wasn't just a record deal, it was the right deal for me. I'm with people I believe in and they believe in me.'

Ten days later, Taylor picked up the phone to him: she had made her decision. It was a yes. She was on board and would become the centrepiece of his new roster of artists.

Taylor signed her contract at a special ceremony at the Country Music Hall of Fame and afterwards they celebrated at The Palm restaurant. As she penned her name, she joked: 'It's kind of like a wedding contract.' Scott hit back, with a serious look on his face: 'No, it's more binding.'

After blood, sweat and tears, Taylor had a record deal. Together with Scott Borchetta, she started hatching a plan that would blow the country music scene away.

CHAPTER THREE

'Seeing how people have rallied behind me like this, it's breathtaking really'

With only one in thousands of new country artists in Nashville successfully cracking the notoriously competitive world, Taylor knew she had lots of arduous work ahead of her. She was just fourteen and the first artist signed to Scott Borchetta's new label, Big Machine Records.

As a rule, country music lent itself to older listeners and women, who preferred listening to the opposite sex singing to them about tragic tales of lost love and the beauty of nature. Taylor's new boss knew what a risk he was taking signing her: his hard-earned reputation was at stake.

'People would look at me cross-eyed [when I told them I was signing Taylor],' Scott told the *New York Times*. 'I would feel like they were deleting me from their Blackberry as I was telling them!'"

Veteran country-music promoter Jerry Bentley told the *Seattle Times*: 'Even if she were twenty-five, the odds would be against her. You have to work 300-plus days for a couple of years and there's no guarantee even then.'

While her critics argued that this genre of music would never appeal to someone younger than twenty-five, Taylor didn't agree. She felt like it could if the subject of the songs were more relevant to the younger age group.

'All the songs I heard on the radio were about marriage and kids and settling down,' she told *Entertainment Weekly*. 'I just couldn't relate to that. I kept writing songs about the guy I dated for a couple of weeks and who cheated on me, about all the things I was going through. There was no reason why country music shouldn't relate to someone my age if someone my age was writing it.'

Even back then, Taylor would spend hours daydreaming about headlining in her own concerts. It felt almost close enough to touch.

'My big dream is to look out into a crowd of thousands of people and have them singing my songs,' she said at the time. 'That to me would be everything I've ever hoped for. I have tunnel vision. And for me that's all I see.'

As part of her learning the ropes of the music world, Scott Borchetta arranged for Taylor to intern at the CMA Music Festival, a four-day event, featuring some of Nashville's most seasoned stars.

She told *Marie Claire* magazine: 'I remember when I was fourteen years old and was holding a clipboard interning at the CMA Music Fest, just feeling like if there was ever a chance that one day people would line up to have me sign something of theirs, then that would be a really, really good day for me.'

Taylor's father, Scott, an astute businessman, invested in the fledgling record company, purchasing 3 per cent of it because he believed his daughter would be a phenomenal success.

'My dad believed in me, even when I didn't,' Taylor said. 'He always knew I could do this. I'm sure that everyone in Reading remembers how much he talked about me. I thought that was sweet, but really I just wasn't as sure it would happen. So, I just love my dad for believing in his little girl.'

Once the excitement of being signed was over, Taylor needed to get down to work in the studio. She had kept many of the songs she had written for Sony so she had lots of material to work with.

'I've been very selfish about my songs,' she revealed to CMT.com. 'I had this dream of this project coming out for so many years that I just stockpiled.'

She presented some of her best efforts to Scott Borchetta, who was starting to get excited about the huge talent he had signed.

Recalling the moment during a Q&A at the CMA Festival in 2012, Scott said when Taylor first played him a song she had written called 'Tim McGraw' he said to her, 'Do you realise what you just wrote? . . . That's your first single'.

Instantly, Scott knew that this would be Taylor's first

single release. He loved the track – it was the perfect angst-ridden song that would resonate with their target audience and he also knew it would bring them some attention from seasoned country listeners by using McGraw's name in the title.

Scott confessed: 'We put that out deliberately so people would ask, "Who's this new artist with a song, 'Tim McGraw'?"'

Taylor started working on her eponymous debut album every day after school and it took just four months to complete. She wrote during every second she had. Her unbelievable work ethic was unparalleled for someone so young.

'I had a double life,' she explained to *Elle* magazine. 'During the day, I walked around, talked to people, went to class, studied for tests, and had crushes on boys and then after school I would go downtown to Music Row in Nashville and I would write songs about those experiences.'

She was also making key decisions about the team of people she worked with. After using some different producers, she persuaded Big Machine to hire Nathan Chapman.

'We switched [album] producers a bunch of times,' Taylor said to CMT.com. 'I started off with this demo producer who worked in a little shed behind this publishing company I was at. His name was Nathan Chapman. I'd always go in there and play him some new songs, and the next week he would have this awesome track, on which he played every instrument, and it sounded like a record. We did this for a period of a year to two years before I got my record deal.

'Then, all of a sudden, it was, "Okay, we're going to use this producer" or "We're going to use that producer." So I got to record with a bunch of really awesome producers in Nashville. But it didn't sound the way that it did with Nathan. He had never made an album before. He had just recorded demos. But the right chemistry hit. Finally, my record label president said, "Okay, try some sides with Nathan."'

Taylor wrote three of the songs on her new album all by herself, including two singles, and co-wrote the other eight with writers, including Liz Rose and two other seasoned writers, Angelo Petraglia and Robert Ellis Orrall. Taylor was very involved in the whole production process and there wasn't one session where they were tracking instruments where she wasn't there; she wanted to completely own the whole song.

'When I write a song I hear how it is supposed to sound in my head,' she said to Sudzin Country website. 'I can hear the production. I can hear what the drums are doing, what the mandolin is doing, what the bass is doing, when I'm writing that song. So usually when we go to the studio all I have to do is sit down with Nathan for ten minutes and say, "This is how I want this to sound" and he puts it all to life.'

Taylor was so excited and impatient about her album's imminent release and set about doing as much as she could to promote it, including setting up her own MySpace page, introducing herself to the world.

Her first blog post talked about how excited she was after doing a showcase for music executives at Scott Borchetta's house; how her parents had bought her a video camera so she could record what she was up to; and how she loved messing around with her band doing voices from the film *Napoleon Dynamite*. She accepted friend requests from new fans, who started to leave her comments and feedback. Slowly, her digital fan base began building and she would spend most of her free time talking to her new followers, who called themselves Swifties.

This kind of viral marketing was almost unheard of in the country music world but Taylor took a really personal approach. This is unusual in itself because generally stars in the music industry employ people to do this on their behalf but not Taylor: she wanted to be firmly in control of her online profile and nothing was off-limits; she spoke to her online followers just as she would to Abigail and her school friends.

'I spend so much time on MySpace,' she elaborated to *Billboard*. 'It's the best way to figure out what your fans and what your friends and these people that helped you get where you are, what they're going through and what they want to hear from you, what they're liking, what they're not. My MySpace is something that I made. The background that you see on there, I went to a Web site and copied the code and copy-and-pasted my "about me" section. I upload all the pictures, I check the comments, I am in charge of everything on that page. It really is important to me and really special to me when someone comes up to me and says, "I'm your friend on MySpace." I've always taken so much pride in it just because it's really personal to me.'

By the time 'Tim McGraw' was released on 19 June 2006, Taylor had had over 2 million hits, and when it hit the airwaves it was downloaded a staggering 500,000 times in less than five months. It was a huge breakthrough single for a new artist.

Speaking to *Entertainment Weekly*, Scott Borchetta talked about MySpace's impact on his new artist's first release.

'People laughed at me. They said, "You're starting a new record label and you signed a 15-year-old female country singer – good for you! You have a teenager – there's a lot of those on country radio. You have a new female artist – there's a lot of those on country radio." They were looking at me like I had two strikes. But I knew we didn't want to count on country radio out of the box. So we went heavy on TV, putting the video out before the single, and doing a special with GAC, and we went heavy on her MySpace and online stuff. By the time we got to country radio, we said: "We have you surrounded and you don't even know it."'

To make a mark on the all-important country charts, Taylor needed radio play. There were only ten employees at Big Machine Records at the time, so Taylor and her mum even sat cross-legged on the floor and helped stuff the CDs in envelopes to send to radio stations. There was no job too small for her.

'With every envelope that I would seal I would look at the address and the station on there and think, "Please, please just listen to this one time,"' she recalled to Reuters. 'I would say a little message to each envelope, "Please, whoever gets this, please listen to this." There's no promise when you're putting out your first single that people are even going to listen to it.'

The 3 minutes and 52 seconds of country pop showed just what Taylor was made of and with hard work brought success: 'Tim McGraw' started to get radio play in late 2006 and, by January the following year, it had edged its way to No. 6 on *Billboard*'s Hot Country Songs chart, eventually staying there for an astonishing 35 weeks. It also peaked at No. 40 on the *Billboard* Hot 100 and eventually went platinum, selling more than a million copies.

The emotive song was received well by the critics, with website AllMusic labelling Taylor 'a talent to be reckoned with,' while online pop magazine *PopMatters* declared the track was 'good enough to recall some of the best country singers of recent years'.

Country-music fans are known for being opposed to new artists and Taylor was warned that she would need to be patient, so she was stunned and delighted when she finally heard her music playing on the radio.

She told *Seventeen* magazine: 'The first time I heard my song on the radio, I was driving down the road and somebody called in and requested it, and I almost drove off the road – literally. My record label president still has the message of me screaming at the top of my lungs, screeching; you can barely hear what I'm saying because I was crying – it was amazing.'

She had also recorded her first music video, which shows her having flashbacks of her boyfriend, who was played by an actor called Clayton Collins. With the young and fun video, and dreamy, heart-on-your sleeve lyrics, it seemed the Taylor had managed to tap into an unknown market: teenage girls who liked country music.

'So many girls come up and say to me, "I have never listened to country music in my life,"' she said. '"I didn't even know my town had a country music station. Then I got your record, and now I'm obsessed." That's the coolest compliment to me.'

As soon as school broke up for the summer, she headed off on a radio tour to promote her new single. Unlike the UK, where traditionally there has been only one big radio station, Radio 1, which means airplay across the country, Taylor needed to go to as many of the 2,500 individual stations across America as she could. There was nothing glamorous about the way they travelled back then; she and her mum hired a rental car and Andrea would drive, while Taylor tried to sleep in the back.

'Radio tours for most artists last six weeks,' she said. 'Mine lasted six months. That's because I wanted it to. I wanted to meet every single one of the people that was helping me out.'

She was so grateful that she even baked cookies for the radio programmers who played her songs and made time for the fans that called in and requested it.

She explained: 'I love it when people want to meet me because I want to meet them! Early on my manager told me, "If you want to sell 500,000 records, then go out there and meet 500,000 people.'

She personally handwrote thank-you notes when radio

stations played her songs, something she continues to do to this day. Her polite outlook didn't go unnoticed. The media were starting to really warm to this bright new star and appreciated her down-to-earth attitude and hard-working ethic. Taylor would listen to what people asked her, giving well thought-out responses.

Leading country interviewer Shannon McCombs explained: '[She's] always friendly, always professional and always tries to put you and everyone else in the room at ease. She's a good interview, too. Some artists just waste your time with their rambling answers but not Taylor. She knows this is her career and she pays attention to detail.'

Life on the road must have been exhausting but Taylor enjoyed every second of it and soon she was being asked to open for other country acts. While she was on the road with her mum, she got a call from the hip country trio Rascal Flatts, who were promoting their album *Me and My Gang*. They asked her to open nine shows for them, with just two days warning, after the previous act Eric Church was fired for playing for too long.

With her usual positive attitude, the young starlet was delighted. Wearing a lucky pair of red cowboy boots, which had a skull and crossbones imprinted on them, she was a natural on stage after so many years playing in bars and festivals, introducing the five separate songs. Her fans held their mobile phones or glowsticks in the air, so they looked like stars in the sky during her rendition of 'Tim McGraw' and she was happy to sign autographs afterwards.

About.com said: 'A lot of times newer, and especially

younger acts haven't learned how to connect with the audience and they seem nervous, or distant. But Taylor exhibited none of that. She talked between songs and took command of the stage with ease.'

She was sweet-natured and polite to everyone. Eric Church told the *Arizona Daily Star*: 'Actually, she called me after I got fired . . . She called and said: "I want you to know that I love what you do." I joked with her, "This is your crowd; they're going to love you. You're going to owe me your first gold record."'He was joking but, when Taylor got her first record, she sent him a note, which read: 'Thanks for playing too long and too loud on the Flatts tour I sincerely appreciate it.'

Talking about her time with Rascal Flatts, Taylor later raved to *Elle Girl* that she was flattered they had asked her to join them:

'I've always been such a fan of their music and it means the world to me that they were the first major artists to take me on the road,' she said. 'When I was sixteen, I barely had a single out and they believed in me enough to let me open up shows with them.'

While some rising stars might take on a huge team of people around them, Taylor liked to be involved at every level. Aside from her mum who travelled with her, she was her own manager and has continued to control every part of her career. She was – and is – the antithesis of a diva, who insists on a whole entourage to trail in her wake.

She told *Harper's Bazaar*: 'When I'm in management meetings when we're deciding my future, those decisions are left up to me. I'm the one who has to go out and fulfil all these obligations, so I should be able to choose which ones I do or not. That's the part of my life where I feel most in control.'

On 24 October, Taylor woke up at 5 a.m. in a New York hotel room. She had butterflies in her tummy and her heart was racing. It was a huge day for her: her debut album hit the shelves and she would be appearing on *Good Morning America*, to play her lead single, 'Tim McGraw'. In between her hectic commitments doing a number of phone interviews with radio stations, she also wanted to find time to walk into a record store and buy her own album.

'I just want to do that and put it on the register face down,' she said. 'I can't even express how excited, slash nervous I am. It's such a cool day because I am in New York City and it feels like that's the place where your album should be released.'

She later starred on a number of different TV shows and to her huge delight, and that of Scott Borchetta and the Big Machine team, Taylor Swift was a hit.

All the tracks on the album had special meanings to Taylor. Alongside 'Tim McGraw', 'Teardrops on My Guitar', 'Picture to Burn', 'The Outside' and 'Our Song' was the plaintive track 'Tied Together with a Smile', which she wrote on the day she learned one of her friends was bulimic.

Taylor told GAC: 'How can somebody that seems so strong have such a horrible, horrible weakness? Something that is killing her?' She continued: 'I always thought that one of the biggest overlooked problems American girls face is insecurity.'

'Mary's Song (Oh My My My)' was inspired by her older neighbours who still seemed really in love, even though they married really young and were in their sixties. She said: 'I thought it was so sweet, because you can go to the grocery store and read the tabloids, and see who's breaking up and cheating on each other (or just listen to my songs, haha). But it was really comforting to know that all I needed to do was go home and look next door to see a perfect example of for-ever.'

The *New York Times* said the album was 'a small master-piece of pop-minded country, both wide-eyed and cynical, held together by Ms. Swift's firm, pleading voice', and web-site AllMusic argued that: 'Taylor Swift's considerably strong voice straddles that precarious edge that both suggests experience far beyond her years and simultaneously leaves no doubt that she's still got a lot of life to live. It's a fresh, still girlish voice, full of hope and naïveté, but it's also a confident and mature one.'

About.com also praised her: 'Taylor Swift is only sixteen years old. But don't let her age fool you! She writes and sings with the passion and conviction of a veteran of country music. She loves what she does, and she gives it her all.'

And *Country Weekly* raved: 'Taylor Swift, 16, beats the jinx – preoccupied with the concerns of a teenage girl, for sure, but demonstrating an honesty, intelligence and ideal-ism with which listeners of any age will be able to connect.'

The album quickly accelerated up the charts, debuting at

No. 19 on the *Billboard* 200. Taylor was overwhelmed and thrilled at the result.

'Sometimes you feel like you have to pinch yourself, it's like, "Am I really here?"' she told *Access Hollywood*.

On her return from the Big Apple, she spent a few much-needed days at home catching up with her friends and relaxing with her family. It had been a whirlwind for her and she had decided that, in order to push herself as far as she could with her music, she couldn't return to school the following year. It was a tough decision and Taylor was sad she wouldn't be seeing her friends every day and gossiping in the classroom.

Taylor's best friend Abigail told *Lawrence Journal World*: 'I mean, any girl knows that if your best friend leaves you in 10th grade, it's just like, "Okay, what do I do now?" So, it was hard for both of us. I had to kind of make a new name for myself around school, and she had to do her own thing out there and miss everything that had been her life for the previous few years. But she just immediately just started doing so well . . . you just couldn't really think about anything else. I just remember she called me one night and we had to have the talk about she's not coming back to school. But after that it was just a way of life and we dealt with it, and we've actually gotten closer since.'

Taylor enrolled in the Aaron Academy, a Christian school, which offered a home-schooling programme. She faced an uphill battle to juggle her music, schoolwork and her friends but she never complained.

'Balancing all this is not hard,' she told *Billboard*. 'I mean what do I have to complain about? I have the best time in the world. I'm so lucky. When I go out in public and I go to a mall, yeah it's a lot different than it was two years ago, but it's a beautiful kind of different. It's the kind of different that I've wanted my entire life. I'm a strong believer that if you work your entire life for something, and you work so hard and you want this one thing so much, you should never complain once you get it.'

Her mum decided that she would travel with Taylor, while her dad would stay at home with Austin. Andrea told Searay website: 'It's a lot of work helping Tay pursue a music career, but it's a lot of fun, too.'

Around this time big brands were cottoning on to Taylor's appeal and she got her first promo jobs, first advertising L.e.i. jeans for Walmart and then she was chosen as the face of Verizon Wireless mobile music campaign, where among other advertising, her face adorned 500,000 bags of popcorn.

Taylor's debut referenced much of her life, and critics and fans would learn that her music would shine a magnifying glass on her secrets. Every guy who she had been involved with must have been feeling giddy with nerves. Taylor was going to get the best form of revenge. In one up-tempo track, 'Should've Said No', she addresses a guy who has cheated on her and she tells him, he 'should've said no' to temptation. She then used a trick that would become a trademark in her albums by coding her CD notes. She didn't mention the boy's name but customised the lyrics in the cover, capitalising letters in each song to pick out the words, 'Sam, Sam, Sam, Sam, Sam.'

'It was only his first name but everyone figured it out,' she confessed to *Women's Health*. 'I'd get texts from him. He was scared out of his mind I'd crucify him on a talk show. All I could think was, "Well you should've said no. That's what the song is about."'

Soon everyone in her hometown was listening in for people and names they knew. Taylor told *Entertainment Weekly*: 'I think it's one of everybody's favourite things to talk about – who my songs are written about. There are definitely a few more people who think that I've written songs about them than there actually are.'

As the media and paparazzi started paying more attention to Taylor's personal life, it soon became clear they would learn more about her through her music than any interviews she may give.

Although she was single at the time, she later explained: 'I write songs about people that I date.' Adding, 'And you'll probably be able to figure out how many breakups I've gone through, how many people I've fallen for – it's very autobiographical.'

Thanks to her hard work, the momentum around her music started to grow and her album climbed in the charts. By November 2006, Taylor had sold 67,000 copies and, in February 2007, the album went gold, meaning it had sold half a million copies. On 21 February, Taylor had a big party. Wearing a low-cut glittering gold dress and her favourite cowboy boots, she celebrated with industry insiders, her school friends and her family at the BMI building in Nashville. As part of the event, she was presented with a huge framed picture containing her CD.

During the pre-party press conference, Scott Borchetta joked: 'Taylor is wearing a gold dress but I am wearing a platinum tie,' referring to the million sales which Taylor aspired to. Talking about signing her when she was just fourteen, he added: 'Still to this day it never hit me that Taylor was a teenager. To me, she was a hit songwriter . . . She never goes anywhere without her guitar.'

Taylor had started back on the road at the start of 2007, this time opening 20 dates for country veteran George Strait, who had amassed over 50 No. 1 hits and sold 62 million albums. Taylor felt very much at home alongside the legend and said she had to keep 'pinching herself' to check it was real.

'The Rascal Flatts tour was a perfect match for me,' she reflected. 'With George Strait, I feel I'm lucky to be in front of a more traditional country audience.' The crowds' reverence for George, she observed, was 'like religion'.

Taylor threw herself into every performance with real passion – be it in a small radio studio with just a few onlookers or in front of a large crowd while opening a tour.

'When you're live people can see it on your face and they can see what the song means to you,' she said. 'I'll never sing one of my songs with a straight face like it means nothing to me because I wrote these songs and they all mean something to me. When you can look at two people in the front row who are singing the words to your songs, I love that. I love to be able to look at someone and make that contact and nod your head and say thanks for being here.'

Everyone loved her positive and fun attitude. The only downside, Scott admitted, was that everyone was shocked by how rapidly she was gaining fans and breaking records.

'My fear is that she'll conquer the world by the time she's 19,' he told the *Washington Post*. 'She'll get to the mountaintop and say: "This is it?" Because she's just knocking down all of these goals that we didn't even have for the first album . . . My job at this point is really to protect her and not burn her out.'

However, far from slowing down, Taylor worked tirelessly, claiming: 'I know it makes me sound like a robot but there is nothing more interesting to me than my career. I feel so lucky to have found something that I love to do so much. I don't have an identity without music.'

She has always been a 'really big worrier', telling the *Daily Mail*: 'I can't believe I get to have the life I have, so I've got a complete fear of messing up, of making a misstep where it all comes crumbling down. It's a high-wire act in my brain all the time.'

She added to *Vogue*: 'I get so ahead of myself. I'm like, "What am I going to be doing at 30?" But there's no way to know that! So it's this endless mind-boggling equation that you'll never figure out. I overanalyse myself into being a big bag of worries.'

As she zigzagged her way across the USA, introducing her songs to new people, slowly 'Taylor Nation' was expanding.

Her followers ranged from older fans of traditional toe-tapping country to younger stars who adored Disney and bubblegum pop, and many others in between. She always remained loyal to her core fan base.

She also became a style icon. Her favourite outfit was a good pair of cowboy boots and a dress, accessorised with delicate jewellery like earrings, bracelets and halo-style headbands, including her trademark leather bracelet with the worlds LOVE LOVE LOVE embossed on it.

'When you wear a dress with cowboy boots, it's kind of a cool irony to the outfit,' she told the *Houston Chronicle*. At that time she revealed that she owned eight pairs of boots and her favourite pair had one boot saying TAYLOR and the other reading SWIFT.

She soon hired the help of stylist Sandy Spika for big events: Sandy helped Taylor decide what to wear and designed a number of original outfits for her. Taylor was always modest about her appearance, telling the *St. Petersburg Times*: 'When I'm going on TV, of course you have the glam squad. They make you look a lot better.'

Unlike typical country singers, Taylor is willowy and natural and she wanted to avoid excessive vanity.

'Country singers don't need fake boobs and big hair,' she said. 'I'm probably the tallest country singer ever . . . and I buy my clothes from Topshop.'

Young girls started to emulate her wholesome and feminine style and Taylor was really flattered.

'I think it's awesome when people talk about the "Taylor Swift look",' she observed during an interview with Country

97.3. 'I think it's really cool when people want to have curly hair and want to wear dresses and boots. That's just what I'm comfortable in. I didn't think I was creating a look or anything.'

Hot on the heels of her blinding album success, in February 2007, Scott Borchetta decided the time was right to release another single and they decided on 'Teardrops on My Guitar', which catapulted up the charts to No. 2 on the *Billboard* Hot Country Songs chart. It became a crossover hit and the video, set in a local Nashville high school and starring a Drew lookalike, Tyler Hilton, was screened on music channel MTV, who traditionally had an aversion to country music. The song became Taylor's highest-charting single from her debut album, hitting the No. 12 spot on the *Billboard* Hot 100. Critics were sold and started to compare her work with that of David Bowie, the Cranberries and Shania Twain.

About.com said: 'Remove the twang of soft country guitar and "Teardrops on My Guitar" is the best teen-pop ballad for quite some time,' while *Billboard* declared: 'The straightforward conversational quality in her lyrics is like hearing a lovelorn confession of a dear friend. The longing in this song is relatable and makes the heart palpable in a moving performance. It's tender, sweet and destined to be another hit.'

Taylor was crossing boundaries and her style was evolving, but she didn't put herself in either category.

'I write songs the way I hear them in my head,' she said. 'Call it what you want ... but the crossover success is wonderful.'

She also received a phone call from the song's star, Drew, who was the inspiration for the song, but Taylor said she was too nervous to call him back. Then, after the song was released, she saw him again. Due to her bad eyesight, she was slow to realise immediately.

'Kellie Pickler and I were going to a hockey game and this guy pulls up,' she told the *Miami Herald*. 'I didn't have my contacts on and didn't see him right away. He's a little older, a little taller, the guy I wrote that song about two and a half years ago. I hadn't talked to him. I didn't know what to say and here he is walking towards me. Everything was nice. There was no, like, screaming and "You're too late!" It was all very cordial.'

In April, she also bumped into some pupils from her old school at a show in her hometown, where she played a mixture of country tracks and pop favourites, backed by a five-piece band of fiddles and banjos.

Talking to the audience, she said: 'When I left three years ago, I had one shot, one opportunity to seize everything I ever wanted. You think I did alright?'

She later told *Teen Vogue* that many of her bullies were in the audience.

'They showed up wearing my t-shirts and asking me to sign their CDs,' she said. 'It made me realize they didn't remember being mean to me and I needed to forget about it too. Really, if I hadn't come home from school miserable every day, maybe I wouldn't be so motivated to write songs. I should probably be thanking them.'

Taylor graduated in 2008 but never went to the school

prom because she was concerned that there were still people there that hated her.

'As supportive as my hometown is, in my high school, there are people who would probably walk up to me and punch me in the face,' she told the *Washington Post*. 'There's a select few that will never like me. They don't like what I stand for. They don't like somebody who stands for being sober, who stands for anything happy. They're going to be negative no matter what. I've had people tell me it would be a security issue if I went back to prom. I hate to go there, but I think it might be true. I heard that when Christina Aguilera went back to her prom, people, like, booed her. I can't imagine going through that. If you know that's going to happen, why put yourself in that situation? I'd rather play for 20,000 screaming people, you know?'

Taylor's first major awards show was the 2007 CMT Music Awards, in April, where she had nominations for Breakthrough Video and Female Video of the Year, both for 'Tim McGraw'. She showed off her fashion credentials in a white dress studded with silver sequins and looked stunning. As her name was announced as the winner for Breakthrough Video, she was bowled over and gave the crowd an awestruck look. Accepting her gong from Carrie Underwood, she gushed: 'I cannot believe this is happening right now. This is for my MySpace people and the fans.'

She couldn't believe she had won, especially a trophy that is voted for by the public and described it as the 'highlight of her year'.

'I can't explain the feeling,' she marvelled to the *Tennessean*. 'I have never been nominated for anything before. I had won nothing before, literally nothing. To have my name called, I didn't know what that was like. I didn't think I was going to get it. When my name was called, I just ran up to the stage at, like, a hundred miles per hour.'

Taylor was genuinely surprised that people liked her so much but the invitations were coming in thick and fast. The following month she attended the prestigious Academy of Country Music Awards, in Las Vegas, where she had a nod for Top New Female Vocalist. The room was packed with her idols and country royalty, including LeAnn Rimes, Kenny Chesney, Faith Hill and Tim McGraw. With her guitar slung over her shoulder, she took to the stage and belted out a heartfelt rendition of 'Tim McGraw' and as she finished she went up to the singer and his wife and introduced herself before hugging them. She lost out on the award to Carrie Underwood, but Taylor didn't care – she finally got to meet the man who inspired her breakthrough single.

'It was just unbelievable,' she told the *Pantagraph*. 'I was performing on stage and it was just me and my guitar. After my song I stepped out and said, "Hi, I'm Taylor." I hadn't met him in the entire year my single had been out. So it was just really cool.' Afterwards, Tim told a radio station that he was delighted she named her debut single after him, laughing: 'It's awesome . . . except I don't know if I should take it as a compliment or I should just feel old!'

Her childlike excitement was infectious and everywhere she went people, famous or otherwise, warmed to Taylor.

Having proved herself during the Rascal Flatts and George Strait tours, Taylor was asked to open for a number of different acts, including Kenny Chesney on his Flip-Flop tour and on Brad Paisley's Bonfires and Amplifiers tour.

Brad personally asked for Taylor to join him after hearing her album. He told *Entertainment Weekly*: 'Taylor Swift was one that I called my manager when I heard her album and said, "We have to get her out on tour." For her to have written that record at 16, it's crazy how good it is. I figured I'd hear it and think, "Well, it's good for 16" – but it's just flat out good for any age.'

She had lots of fun on the road with her fellow artists Jack Ingram and Kellie Pickler. The three of them got up to all sorts of mischief and pranks while they were away.

Taylor told website Just Jared: 'Going out on the Brad Paisley tour, that was a notorious tour for pranking. Before I went out on tour, I knew that he pranked a lot of his opening acts a lot towards the end of the tour. I was out on the road with Kellie Pickler and Brad and we became best friends, Kellie and I, and we decided that we were gonna start pranking him the first week. He had a brand-new song out then called "Ticks", so Kellie and I ordered these huge, gigantic, full body tick costumes and dressed up in them and ran out on stage during his performance of that song. And then we had the other opening act – Jack Ingram – come out dressed up like an insect killer guy with the mask and the spray gun and everything and he proceeded to come out on stage and spray us and kill us. It was great; it was really fun. We have it on video and that's definitely my favourite moment of the tour.'

Taylor declared that she adored touring, saying it 'kept her sane'.

'Honestly, when I come home I literally just don't know what to do with myself, because I feel I should be doing a meet and greet line or doing something,' she told *UnRated Magazine*.

Later in the year, she was even asked on Tim McGraw and Faith Hill's joint Soul 2 Soul tour.

Life was getting better and better. In June, Taylor and her family drove to the convention centre in Nashville for what they thought was another gold record presentation but, to her great surprise, instead of a gold plaque she was handed a platinum one, meaning her record had sold over a million copies.

When she saw it, she turned to Scott and joked: 'You liar!' much to the delight of the people watching. She was completely overwhelmed.

'I would have been happy to get another gold record, but it was a platinum record,' she marvelled to musiccity-moms.net. 'It's the most beautiful thing that I think I've ever seen in my life. When I was a little kid, I went to a Kenny Chesney concert and just thought, "If I can have a platinum album, I'll be set and I'll be satisfied with what I've done." It's just crazy to think that in just under eight months we were able to go platinum. Eight months is not a very long time at all. Seeing how people have rallied behind me like this, it's breathtaking really.'

Eventually, her debut album amassed over 5 million sales. After 63 weeks on the *Billboard* 200, on the week ending 19

January 2008, the album reached its peak at No. 5 due to sales of 47,000 copies. By late 2012, the album had stayed on the chart for 267 weeks. The artist marked the longest stay on the *Billboard* 200 by any album released in the decade.

This was just one of many, many incredible records that Taylor would break.

CHAPTER FOUR

'I think if you put out one song and one person likes it, you're automatically a role model whether you like it or not . . .'

By July 2007, Taylor had amassed a staggering 20 million hits on her MySpace site and the fan base was multiplying by the day. She understood her fans and they loved her and her heartfelt music. When it came to the world of country music, the pop princess was like a breath of fresh air and her fans connected with her instantly: she just got them.

Taylor said: 'I think one of the cool things about this is that MySpace is one of the main reasons why I'm here, along with radio and word of mouth. And MySpace is pretty much a younger thing at the moment . . . So yeah, definitely, it's bringing a completely different audience to country music. And I am so grateful for that.'

As the fans demanded more material she released 'Our Song', the third single from the album, on 22 August. She had written the up-tempo anthem at school in just twenty minutes and it was one of her favourites.

'When we were picking songs for the album, I stood by this one and made sure it got recorded. I just knew there was something about it,' she told GAC. 'I think there's some sort of magic in the way the track sounds like it's bouncing, almost!'

It rose to No. 1 in the country charts before the end of the year and stayed put for six weeks, making Taylor the youngest person to ever single-handedly write a chart-topping country hit. It also went to No. 16 on the pop chart, with its broad crossover appeal. She was astonished and happy in equal measures, but remained humble when talking about it.

'I wanted a song that would make people tap their feet,' Taylor explained to the *Washington Post*. 'I got that and a whole lot more! A No. 1 single for six weeks! Whatever! No big deal!'

The fourth and fifth singles released through 2007 and 2008 – 'Picture to Burn' and 'Should've Said No' respectively – were also popular with fans – peaking at No. 3 and No. 1 respectively in the country chart. Taylor was on a roll.

She continued to tour extensively promoting the album and also participated in meet-and-greet sessions with her fans, where she amazed her team with her uncanny ability to remember fans she had met previously.

Rick Barker of Big Machine Records, told website Pollstar: 'One of the things that Taylor is insistent upon is that [the fans] are not rushed. They obviously can't spend five or ten minutes individually, but she never wants to make them feel like it's a cattle call.'

After her experience of meeting her idols as a child, Taylor wanted to do something distinct and she made sure she put time aside in her busy schedule, unlike other artists.

She said: 'It's always been really important to me because I've been that kid standing in that autograph line with my mum.'

Taylor, who now often spends up to fifteen hours at a time talking to fans via social networks, said that rather than call her followers 'fans' she likes to refer to them as 'friends' because she wants to be in their lives as much as she is in theirs.

Talking to the the *Daily Telegraph*, she explained: 'I've met many of the girls more than once . . . I have girls come up to me and tell me exactly what's going on in their love lives. They always come out with these bold confessions like, "I'm so glad I'm at your concert tonight. My boyfriend just left me . . ."'

On one occasion, she even followed a girl in her local town, who she saw wearing a t-shirt with her face on.

'I was driving near the mall and I saw this girl with my tour t-shirt on,' she told *Parade* magazine. 'She was probably eleven. I made a U-turn and tried to follow her. I really had to do some manoeuvring. I found her in a video game store and just kind of walked up and said, "Oh, hi, I wanted to meet you." She had no idea what to say for about three minutes. Then her mom walked over, burst into tears and proceeded to tell me that they'd driven all the way from Austin, Texas, to see where I was discovered.'

Taylor seemed to take fame in her stride and loved hugging, calling herself 'one of life's huggers' and having her picture taken with her hoards of adoring fans.

Andrea told ew.com: 'She can't go now to a store without having people come up to her – which she loves. It makes her day when she's gone somewhere and people have come up to her and said, "I love your music – can I take a picture?" She's always grabbing the camera and going, "Come here" and getting the MySpace shot, holding the camera and posing together. She likes that attention.

'I think where she differs from some people who get to that spot and realise that they don't really like their privacy sort of being restricted – well, for her that's not an issue. But she never in her life ever said, "I want to be famous" or "I want to be rich" or "I want to be a star." Those words absolutely never came out of her mouth. If they had, I would have said, "Honey, maybe you're doing it kind of for the wrong reasons."

'For her, the happiest I ever see her is just after she's written a killer song. As a parent, I felt really good about that. If that's where she draws happiness from, she'll have that the rest of her life.'

Taylor's generous spirit extended to her performances. In

August 2007, she sang 'Teardrops on My Guitar' live on the season final of *America's Got Talent* when 14-year-old finalist Julienne Irwin requested to duet with her. The youngster told a country-music blog: 'Taylor Swift could not have embraced me more. She treated me as though we had been friends our entire lives.'

The plaudits kept rolling in and she was genuinely shocked at each win, which endeared her to new people. In October, her songwriting peers at the Nashville Songwriters Association International honoured her with their esteemed Songwriter/Artist of the Year Award, tied with country stalwart Alan Jackson, making her the youngest artist ever to receive it.

As she clasped her prize, she said: 'The fact that this award is voted on by my songwriting peers – I don't even know how to explain how honoured I feel. I mean, I was just sitting at the table and they called Alan Jackson's name and I'm just like, "Oh, my God, that's awesome!" And then all of a sudden they say my name and I'm like, "What happened?" I'm so humbled by this experience. It's just so unbelievable.'

The fans couldn't get enough of Taylor's music and in October she got into the festive spirit early by releasing a holiday album, *Sounds of the Season: The Taylor Swift Holiday Collection*. Featuring holiday classics such as George Michael's 'Last Christmas' and Bing Crosby's 'White Christmas' alongside original songs, it failed to have the success of her debut album but still hit No. 46 on the *Billboard* 200 chart. In addition to this new offering, she also released a special deluxe version of her original album. She had wanted to put out another album but her record label insisted it was too soon and compromised by allowing her to add some new songs to her debut.

She told music.aol.com: 'The album has been out for a year, but it's too early to put out the second studio album. But we wanted to give [the fans] more music. So this was an opportunity to put out three new songs and a bunch of exclusive content. I actually edited a home movie on the laptop, and it's on there as a specials feature.'

She worked so hard and wanted to give her fans everything they asked for.

By November, Taylor had been on the road for almost a year and said she felt like she had seen so much and grown up during that time.

'It definitely rounds you as a human,' she remarked to the *Toronto Star*. 'I feel like I've already gone to college . . . as far as being away from home, having to learn how to survive, having to learn so many different things about the industry and meeting different people you've never met before.'

She was also aware of how much she was growing as an artist. Singing on stage had become second nature to her.

'I think this is one of the professions that you really have to learn by doing it,' she said during a TV interview. 'You don't learn how to not have stage fright by hearing someone giving you advice about it. You learn to not have stage fright by getting up on stage three hundred times in a row to the point where it feels like you're standing in your bedroom, singing to the mirror.'

However, her schedule was hectic but she showed no sign of slowing down.

Speaking to About.com, she said: 'Right now is when I'm able to go on the road as much as possible. My label has always been so great to let me choose what I do with my time. Whether I want to have a lot of days off or what I want to do. When given the option for days off, I've always said no, because I want to go out there and meet people. And see people and perform. Because what else is there for me to do to ensure this lasts. Touring is totally where I am right now.'

She added that she was always striving for the next goal and she was still dreaming of starring in her own spectacular headline show.

'I want to be a headliner some day,' she said. 'I want have people come out and see a show where I play an hour and a half. I'm so excited about so many things down the line.'

That month, she attended the Country Music Association (CMA) Awards – known as the Oscars of the country music world – dressed in a stunning metallic floor-length gold dress with a flowing skirt. After changing into a short, black sequinned dress, black tights and long black gloves similar to the outfit she wore in the video, she belted out 'Our Song'.

But nothing could top the next moment, when she picked up the coveted Horizon Award, which is given to a new country singer or group that has left a lasting impact on the industry. Previous winners have included the Dixie Chicks and Carrie Underwood. It solidified her position as country music's most successful rising star.

'I can't believe that this is real,' she said during her emotional acceptance speech, when she struggled to convey her happiness. 'I want to thank God and my family for moving to Nashville so I could do this, and I also want to thank country radio. I will never forget the chance you took on me. Brad Paisley, thank you for letting me tour with you. Scott Borchetta, everybody at Big Machine Records, and the fans – you have changed my life. I can't even believe this. This is definitely the highlight of my senior year.'

The wheels of fame were firmly rolling and the recognition of Taylor's music kept growing. On 6 December, Taylor was called upon to help announce the Grammy nominations and, at just seventeen, was the youngest artist on stage.

Foo Fighters' Dave Grohl took to the podium to announce the nominations in the category of Best New Artist, an accolade given to celebrated artists such as the Beatles, Alicia Keys, Sheryl Crow and LeAnn Rimes in the past – and Taylor was ecstatic to hear her own name. This was a huge achievement for any artist on the music scene, let alone one who was still only seventeen and who had roots in the country music world. She squealed before hugging her fellow announcers and Dave said: 'Don't worry, Taylor, you got it in the bag.'

'It's so unbelievable,' she told the *Houston Chronicle*. 'That's an all-genre category, and there's certainly no obligation to have a country artist in that category.'

Eventually, troubled singer Amy Winehouse triumphed but Taylor was overjoyed to receive a nomination and she worked the red carpet like a professional, dressed in a strapless purple gown with leaf detailing. She did get the chance to make her Grammys debut and presented an award to Rihanna and Jay-Z for the Best Rap/Sung Collaboration for 'Umbrella', a song that would later be one of her favourite songs to cover in her concerts.

On 13 December, Taylor turned eighteen. In the morning, she lay in bed in her pyjamas and registered to vote; her friends teased her that this was the craziest thing she would do. She hung out with her pals and had her hair and nails done in preparation for her a pink-themed party in Nashville. Two hundred guests turned out to the bash and Taylor wowed the crowd in a hot pink Betsey Johnson dress.

Andrea told *People* magazine: 'This party is our birthday gift to her. She knows the real gifts in life are relationships.'

When she was asked what the best part of turning eighteen was, Taylor replied: 'I wanted a No. 1 record and I got that and I got something I didn't even ask for: a Grammy nomination. It's been a great year.'

Among the guests was country star and former *American Idol* contestant Kellie Pickler, who Taylor had grown increasingly close to since they toured together alongside Brad Paisley.

'She's like a sister,' Taylor told the *Reading Eagle*. 'People say we're such opposites, but that's what makes us such good friends. She's incredibly blunt. I love that about her.'

Kellie, three years Taylor's senior, admitted she felt very protective of the young starlet, telling website The Boot: 'I officially adopted her as my little sister. She's so smart. She's very talented . . . It's good to be on the road with friends.

This business can be very lonely, because we're always on the go.'

Taylor's friendship with Kellie also made her realise how lucky she was to have such supportive parents and it was occasions like this that really drove it home to her.

'I know I'm so lucky that I've got two perfect parents,' she told the *Washington Post*. 'I'm really good friends with Kellie, whose mom abandoned her. I looked at my mom, who's been there for everything and I think, like, if I'd been in Kellie's situation, I probably wouldn't have made it. I look at other people who have absentee fathers or self-consumed mothers and I'm so lucky ... my mom is my best friend. She's been there for me when no one else has. And she's never been afraid of telling me the honest truth.'

After Kellie helped Taylor to blow out her candles, the boss of her music label Scott Borchetta gave her a super-sized Barbie-pink Chevrolet pick-up truck. Within days of receiving it, she gave the truck to a charity which organises holidays for terminally ill children.

'My label were so awesome and gave me this amazing truck,' she said. 'The moment I saw it I knew the kids would love it. They have camps all over the country for kids who are sick. It's one week each summer they forget they're sick and just have a blast and hang out with people they can relate to. They look forward to it and I love that cause.'

This was just the start of Taylor's philanthropic work, giving much of her money away to causes close to her heart.

After her party, Taylor was more than happy to relax at home over Christmas and celebrate her unprecedented success: she had become one of the biggest acts of the year but it still wasn't enough for her. Her stamina knew no bounds.

'I love having a goal, feeling like I'm on a mission,' she said. 'I love trying to beat what I've done so far.'

In January 2008, Taylor joined Alan Jackson on his Like Red on a Rose tour and then in March went back on tour with Rascal Flatts in Canada. She was working hard on her next album and had been writing while she was on the road.

Talking to website SongwriterUniverse, she explained: 'I've written a lot of songs by myself lately, especially since I've been alone so much on the road. I do love writing on the road – I usually write at the concert venue. I'll find a quiet place in some room at the venue, like the locker room.'

At this time, she mostly composed her new songs on her guitar, rather than the piano.

'You know, I'll be sitting in my room and I'll get an idea for a song and I'll just grab my guitar and start adlibbing,' she told website Just Jared. 'I think that when you write a song on piano it gives you a different feel. I'm not the best piano player but I do know chords and I do know how to play and how to write a song on piano. It's really fun for me to get to switch that up every once in a while and there are a few songs on the new record that I wrote on piano.'

She also said that she always wrote the lyrics and the melodies of her hits together, explaining to CMT: 'Lyrics and melody are married. Hand in hand, synchronic, I write it all together. Sometimes after I've written a song and I'm thinking about it, a line will hit me that will suit better than the original, so I'll change it, or I'll come up with a line I want to repeat in the bridge. Song ideas never hit me at the same place or the same time of day. I might awake at 2 a.m. in my bunk on the bus with a song idea, and I wipe my sleepy eyes and write.'

In February 2008, Taylor bought her own huge tour bus off singer Cher and took great pleasure in kitting it out in her own lush and girly style with a brown velvet couch, blonde laminated panelling, an electric fireplace, with a champagne marble surround, a treadmill, a huge bed piled high with silky turquoise and brown cushions, with her first two multi-platinum albums above it. A brass sign above the entrance read 'Never never never give up'.

The new home for Team Taylor when they were on the road didn't come cheap, the singer told Just Jared.

'I think my biggest splurge so far has been my tour bus. If I'm spending money, it's gonna be putting it back into my career. I don't like to be extravagant any other place. My tour bus is really important because I live there. I'm there more than when I'm home. So, I put a fireplace on my tour bus and a flip-down treadmill and a really comfortable bed. I feel like I'm home whenever I'm on my tour bus. I do not regret that splurge.'

On her bus, she stocked up on all her favourite treats such as Starbucks coffee, cans of Diet Coke, Cinnamon Toast Crunch and strawberry Pop-Tarts, along with her most important possessions.

She told GAC: 'Some of my must-have items are make-up – I love make-up. It's not that I absolutely need it, but I really like it. I think it's fun. It's like art class.' She also loved watching make-up tutorials on YouTube in rare moments of relaxation. She always found it hard to switch off and always wanted to know what was next in her schedule.

'Also I like my cell phone just because I like keeping in touch with people. I always have to be knowing exactly what's going on with my career at that moment. I'm always bothering my record label – "Hey! What's going on today? What are we working on?" I am really annoying.'

She also listened to other artists' music and not just country music. Eminen, Kanye West, John Mayer, Maroon 5 and Coldplay all featured on her iPod. In her down time, she amused herself by watching her favourite TV shows, *Grey's Anatomy*, *Teen Mom* and *CSI*, on the state-of-the art TV and sound system on the bus.

Her mum was always with Taylor but there was only one thing they bickered about.

'This is going to sound horrible but the only real argument I have with my mom is, the temperature on the tour bus,' Taylor lamented. 'She likes it freezing, and I don't. I like the bus really, really hot. So usually, she'll turn the bus temperature all the way down to 65 and be like, "Taylor! You've got to stop turning it up?" And I'll be like, "Okay, mom." When she turns around to walk away I'll turn it back up to 80. Then she'll come back and be like, "Taylor!" So those are the only real arguments we get in. My mom and I get along and my dad and I get along really well so it's gotten to the point where all we argue about is stupid stuff.'

*

Unlike so many stars, Taylor didn't court headlines about her private life while she was on the road and her fame escalated. While many stars would have gone crazy with their new wealth and fame and gone down the road of drink and drugs, Taylor was determined to stay the down-to-earth and innocent girl she had always been.

She told the *Washington Post*: 'I'm not perfect, but I've never done anything wrong, like, criminal record-wise, or like my mum screaming at me really loudly-wise. Okay, sometimes my room isn't clean. She'll come in and say, "Taylor, you're still a teenager living under my roof, you still need to clean your room." But I've never been a party girl. I'd rather sit at home and bake on a Friday night than go to parties.

'In high school, all my friends would go out drinking and stuff but I never, ever wanted to let my parents down. And I never want to let my fans down. I never want to let those little girls I see in the front row down by doing something stupid that's, like, completely preventable and completely my fault. When people go through drug problems and alcohol problems, everyone points their finger at them and says: "You did this to yourself." I don't want to be that girl.'

Taylor has always been aware of her behaviour and once admitted to *Vogue* that if she ever does lose it, 'I usually spend the next four days apologizing.'

'I get post-conversation anxiety,' she said. 'I am so sorry if I said something weird. Did I make that weird? I am sorry if I made that weird!'

She explained that when she was younger she always

looked at her idols and what they said, wore and what their opinions were. She was embracing her new role-model status. It was something that she was not going to take lightly.

'I think if you put out one song and one person likes it, you're automatically a role model whether you like it or not,' she said to Country 97.3. 'You can choose to ignore it or choose to accept it. I embrace it. I like it. I think it's really cool when someone comes up and says, "You're a really great role model for my daughter." It's a compliment about my music, it's a compliment about my character and when someone compliments your character, how can you not love that?'

The new 'little miss perfect' seemed like the flawless antidote to the more fast-living stars like Britney Spears and Lindsay Lohan who had fallen from grace and were often in the headlines for their turbulent private lives and public struggles with drink and drugs. Those who were waiting for Taylor to be ruined by fame and fortune and tumble off her angelic pedestal would be sadly disappointed.

She told the *Daily Mail*: 'I've been given the freedom to do whatever I want . . . if I want to storm out of the house and go to a club and get drunk and take my clothes off and run naked through Nashville, I can do that. I just really would rather not. It's as simple as that.

'It's not like I've been beaten down by some corporation that's forcing me to always behave myself – I just naturally do. Sometimes people are fascinated by the fact that I don't care about partying; almost to the point where they think it's weird. I think when we get to the point where it's strange for you to not be stumbling around high on something . . . it's a warped world.'

She added that she wanted to pay back some of her family and friends' belief in her.

She said: 'When you lose someone's trust, it's lost, and there are a lot of people out there who are counting on me right now.'

Financial success also wasn't going to go to her head. She had saved her money from her first job and bought herself a champagne-coloured Lexus car, which she still owns, and she started to make shrewd investments, helped by her father.

'Ever since I was a little kid, my dad has been telling me to save money or invest in utilities, 'cos my dad is a stock-broker,' she told her fans during an online Q&A. Her father even used to joke and, whenever someone said, 'Bye-bye,' he would hit back, 'Buy bonds!' 'And he lives and breathes it. My dad is so passionate about what he does, like in the way I'm passionate about music.'

Her publicist's phone was ringing off the hook as magazine editors requested her as their covergirl. In April, she graced the front cover of *Blender* magazine dressed in tight leather trousers and a sharp white tee.

Talking about dating, she said: 'I just don't have the time,' adding that she hadn't even kissed a boy for over two years. When asked about her dream prom date, she said it would be gossip columnist Perez Hilton, who affectionately called her T-Swizzle.

'Your prom date is supposed to be fun and hilarious, and I think I'd have more fun with Perez than with anyone else,' she said.

She proved that she had made her mark in the world of celebrity when she was put on *People* magazine's Most Beautiful People list. Then in June, she made it to the cover of *Seventeen*.

'It's a huge dream come true for me. Since middle school, I subscribed to *Seventeen*. Every single month I would see who was on the cover and I was like, "God, I wish this was me!"'

The plaudits kept rolling in. Also in April, Taylor attended the CMT Awards for the second time and picked up prizes voted for by the fans, for Video of the Year and Female Video of the Year, both for 'Our Song'. The crowd admired her raspberry-coloured Balenciaga dress, but bizarrely, she was barefoot.

She explained to *People*: 'I walked by Faith Hill and I was like, "This hurts so bad." And she was like, "Take them off." Faith Hill told me to. So I did it.'

In May, she graced the red carpet at the Academy of Country Music Awards and after picking up the Top New Female Vocalist gong and dedicating it to her mum, she performed 'Should've Said No' and wowed the crowd by throwing her guitar to one side and performing under falling rain, which poured from the ceiling. The audience took to their feet to applaud her. It was a defining moment for her: proving to everyone just how she was ready to compete with some of the world's biggest stars.

*

By June, her album had gone triple platinum and people would constantly ask when the next album was coming out. Big Machine did know they had to keep her new legion of fans happy, so she released a CD, *Beautiful Eyes*, which was sold exclusively in Walmart shops from July, featuring six new tracks, different versions of the songs from her debut and DVD of unseen footage, including an interview and some backstage videos. She also adopted a shrewd marketing ploy and put a cap on the number that were released.

Taylor told GAC: 'I'm only letting my record company make a small amount of these. The last thing I want any of you to think is that we are putting out too many releases. I'm not going to be doing a bunch of promotion for it because I don't want there to be confusion about whether it's the second album or not. I've gotten so many emails for people asking for new songs, and I thought this might tide them over till the new album comes out in the fall.'

Beautiful Eyes did far better than Big Machine had anticipated, sailing straight to the top spot on the Country Albums chart, pushing her first album into second place, making her the first album to own the top two chart positions together since LeAnn Rimes in 1997.

Taylor was elated with her continuing success and carried on playing back-to-back concerts with her pink guitar slung over her shoulder. She wasn't following anyone else's path and would do her own thing, belting out her own country hits and breaking into spine-tingling acoustic versions of pop artists' best records. Her plan to do something different from other stars was working.

Louisa Jepson

'You know I'm not really looking to model my career on anyone,' she noted. 'I want to do everything new. I mean country music will always be country music . . . but the audiences have changed and expanded. I think it would be great if when I'm ninety years old and looking back on life, I can say I did things people didn't expect and was successful.'

She had proved the doubters and her critics wrong: Taylor Swift was no passing wonder; she was here to stay.

CHAPTER FIVE

'I'm not even going to remember the boy who broke up with me over the phone in 27 seconds when I was eighteen'

Any guy who wanted to date Taylor Swift , be he famous or otherwise, now knew he was fair game when it came to being written about in one of her biting songs.

In the summer of 2008, she netted her first famous man, Joe Jonas, one of the Jonas Brothers. The three brothers from New Jersey – Joe, Nick and Kevin – were making a huge impact on the teen pop scene. They were schooled by their mum and their dad was a pastor; they are deeply religious and have made a vow of chastity until marriage, wearing symbolic purity rings.

Taylor had said that she was keen to date someone in

the industry, 'who gets what you do and gets that you're not going to be around a lot'. And with their hugely successful careers, cute-as-a-button looks and clean-living outlooks, Taylor and Joe looked like a match made in music heaven.

The pair were first rumoured to be a couple when she attended one of their concerts in California in July and while they both denied it, the gossip kept mounting. The young lovebirds were also seen eating ice cream together near Taylor's home in Hendersonville and he was seen backstage at one of her gigs at West Palm Beach that August, standing alongside her dad Scott.

'He only watched her performance, then walked backstage to the meet and greet area,' a source told *People* magazine. 'But when he saw people start to recognize him, he hid. It was real obvious he didn't want people to know he was there to see Taylor.'

Taylor was also given a cameo role in the trio's film, *Jonas Brothers: The 3D Concert Experience*, performing 'Should've Said No', and joined the boys filming in Columbus Circle in New York.

When radio host Ryan Seacrest put Joe, who is a couple of years Taylor's senior, on the spot and asked about the romance, Joe couldn't lie because of his religious beliefs. Instead, he diplomatically replied: 'She's a great girl. I think anybody would love to go on a date with her.' When Taylor was asked in an interview about Joe, she responded in a similar way, saying: 'He's an amazing guy and anybody would be lucky to date him,' suggesting that they had put their heads together to come up with a suitable reply to the inevitable questions.

Neither Taylor nor Joe's people confirmed the relationship but Joe's management were keen for him to appear single to his fans, which is fairly common for young heart-throbs in the public eye. The couple must have gone out of their way to outwit the media to meet in secret but sources said the romance seemed solid.

The songstress was starting to be asked more personal questions but she refused to discuss Joe's promise ring. When *Philly* magazine asked her if it was a deal-breaker, she responded carefully: 'I don't ever talk about how I feel about that sort of thing because it makes people look at me sexually, which has never been a goal of mine. So, honestly, deal-breaker? That's actually a plus for me.'

Perhaps due to the nature of both parties' never-ending tours and personal commitments, the relationship fell apart a few months later, when Joe apparently ended their romance by phone. Soon afterwards, he started dating actress Camilla Belle, who appeared in his video for the single 'Lovebug'.

But rather than take the split lying down, Taylor's comments would be reported widely. When she was asked by *OK!* magazine about the break-up, she revealed in a show-stopping statement: 'They've been together for months. That's why we broke up.' Clearly, she felt Joe had given into temptation.

Taylor later spoke of the split to Ellen DeGeneres and said: 'It's all right – I'm cool. You know what, it's like, when I find that person that is right for me, he'll be wonderful. When I look at that person, I'm not even going to remember the boy who broke up with me over the phone in 27 seconds when I was eighteen.'

She also posted a video for her forthcoming album and among the promo material she was seen holding up a Joe Jonas doll and saying, 'See, this one comes with a phone so he can break up with other dolls.' A few scenes later, she held up a doll of herself and said, 'Stay away from him, okay?'

It seemed Taylor's flawless image was cracking under the spotlight and she was even forced to deny pregnancy rumours on her MySpace page, writing: 'I read a very creative rumour this morning saying I'm pregnant, which is the most IMPOSSIBLE thing on the planet. Take my word for it. Impossible.'

The gossip magazines and Internet sites had a field day with Taylor's revelations and, by November, Joe felt he needed to hit back at the rumours of infidelity and wrote an open letter to his fans to try to repair some of the damage.

He penned: 'Several things I will state with all my heart . . . I never cheated on a girlfriend. It might make someone feel better to assume or imply I have been unfaithful but it is simply not true. Maybe there were reasons for a break-up. Maybe the heart moved on. Perhaps feelings changed. I am truly saddened that anything would potentially cause you to think less of me.'

As for that 27-second phone call, he added: 'I called to discuss feelings with the other person. Those feelings were obviously not well received. I did not end the conversation. Someone else did. Phone calls can only last as long as the person on the other end of the line is willing to talk.'

He concluded: 'There were later attempts at communication that had no response. I wish the best for the other person but could not sit back any longer and leave our fans with a wrong impression of the truth.'

Soon after, there were rumours that Taylor was 'cold' and 'frigid' and that's why the romance ended. Whatever the real story, the singer made it clear she was in no hurry to replace Joe with another man.

Speaking to radio station KIIS FM, she said: 'I'm trying to shake it off. I'm not ready to jump back into anything with anybody because I don't think that would be fair to them . . . if I tried to find someone to fill the void right now.'

She explained that she enjoyed her own company and liked being single.

'I'm not typically the girl who dates a lot of guys or is in relationships a lot,' she told The Boot. 'Most of my life, I've been single. If I meet somebody who's great, I'll make an exception. But I'm really happy being alone . . . I don't feel a sense of emptiness if I don't have a boyfriend.'

However, after being hurt by Joe, she devised a new set of dating rules for herself to make sure she ended up with the right guy.

'I have this rule: I don't call a guy first. And you can't ever send two text messages in a row. If you're like, "I need to talk to you" all the time, [or] "Why didn't you call me back?" . . . If you're that girl, then nobody's going to want to date you.'

With her heartbreak so fresh, she went home and did what she knows best and composed a new revenge song,

'Forever and Always', about a boyfriend who starts to drift away from her and she doesn't know why. Describing her new track, she said: 'It's a song about watching somebody completely fade away and wondering what you did wrong.'

The song, which saw Taylor 'basically screaming because I'm so mad', included a verse which asked whether she'd been out of line, or said something too honest that made him run and hide.

She said: 'I've written about it, and I like to write about my life. That's just how I deal with things.'

With the finishing touches being made to her second album, Taylor 'absolutely begged' for the single to be added to the finished release, which led to some testing times for the music production team who had to work around the clock to make sure it was included.

Scott Borchetta told *E! True Hollywood Story*: 'Here's the deal. We have to go in, cut the track, you have to sing it and we have to send it out the next day.'

Taylor found it a thrill to be challenged and later explained: 'I think it's fun ... knowing that two days before you're scheduled to have the last master in and everything finished and they're ready to go print up the booklets, I can write something, call my producer, we can get in the studio, put a rush on it, get an overnight mix and that can be a last-minute addition to the record.'

With the battle lines firmly drawn, Joe then appeared to write his own revenge ballad in response, called 'Paranoid', on his album *Lines, Vines and Trying Times*.

There was absolutely no reading between the lines; the track even specifically referred to Taylor's track, 'Teardrops on My Guitar'. When Joe was asked about it he told MTV: 'We went through a lot in the past year and a half, all of us. And you're just going to have to get the record and figure it out for yourself.'

Much later he told *Details* magazine: 'I think all artists have a right to write about what happens to them. But I have a right to write about things too . . . Break-ups, hurts. Me hurting somebody and feeling bad about it . . . I think there's a lot of scenarios where people might wanna hear my side of the story.'

Taylor knew that releasing her second album would be more challenging than the first. The runaway success of her debut was brilliant but could just be seen as a lucky break by a young star who had written a few catchy songs. And while the first album was created from material she had written over a number of years, the follow-up would be produced during an intense period of touring, promotions and interviews. In order to have longevity, she knew she would have to wow both the critics and her fans once again. It was the ultimate showcase of her talent.

The album's lead single, 'Love Story', was released on 12 September 2008 to a cheering fanfare of reviews. Inspired by a love interest of hers that wasn't popular with her friends and family, she likened her situation to that of Shakespeare's Romeo and Juliet. However, rather than a tragic ending, she gave the dreamy song a happy one.

She told CMT.com: 'This isn't a fairytale, it's Shakespeare, but Romeo and Juliet were always my favourite couple because they didn't care, and they loved each other no matter what. And it was always my favourite – except for the ending. So with 'Love Story', I just took my favourite characters and gave them the ending that they deserve.'

However, she also hinted at the fact it was written from personal experience and opened up about how hard it was to have a relationship when she was so busy and in the spotlight.

'I used to be in high school where you see [a boyfriend] every day,' she told the *Los Angeles Times*. 'Then I was in a situation where it wasn't so easy for me and I wrote this song because I can relate to the whole Romeo and Juliet thing.'

Drawing on her love of fables, Taylor was still dreaming of her fairy-tale ending, explaining to *Teen Vogue*, 'the "Marry me Juliet, I love you" is I think every girl's fantasy ending and the ending I hope I have someday'.

She admitted that, like some of her other successful hits, she dreamt up the heart-warming, romantic track very quickly in her pink and purple-decorated bedroom.

'Most of the time, songs that I write end up being finished in thirty minutes or less,' she explained to *Time* '"Love Story" I wrote on my bedroom floor in about twenty minutes. When I get on a roll with something, it's really hard for me to put it down unfinished.'

The song won rave reviews for its composition and writing and did well outside America, which is a rare occurrence for new artists. It rocketed to No. 2 in the UK and No. 1 in Australia. Eventually, it sold more than 8 million copies worldwide, becoming one of the best-selling singles of all time.

The video, which showed Taylor in elegant period dress with a backdrop of a fairytale castle and a beautiful sunset alongside hot actor Justin Gaston, also won plaudits, with *Entertainment Weekly* comparing Taylor's acting to that of Hollywood darling Keira Knightley. Taylor had to pinch herself yet again.

It was a good omen for *Fearless*, which hit the shelves on 11 November 2008. Taylor made a midnight appearance at her local Hendersonville Walmart, signing autographs as copies flew off the shelves and thanking her fans for their dedication and loyalty.

As with her debut she wrote or co-wrote all thirteen tracks and she also made her debut as a record producer, co-producing all the tracks alongside Nathan Chapman.

Marking another baby step towards a more pop and commercial offering, Taylor commented to the *Oakland Press*: 'It's the same kind of album I made [in 2006] – just two years older. Sound-wise, it's the kind of songs I like to write, which are country songs, but I guess because of the subject matter and because of some of the melodies I love to use, I guess they have crossover appeal. I like to think of it more as spillover, because I'm a country artist and I write country songs, and I'm lucky enough to have them played on pop radio.'

Again, the album included songs about love and

relationships and Taylor joked that her boyfriends had been warned that they might be included.

Talking about why she decided to call it *Fearless*, she explained in the notes:

To me, Fearless is not the absence of fear. It's not being completely unafraid. To me, Fearless is having fears, Fearless is having doubts. Lots of them. To me, Fearless is living in spite of those things that scare you to death. Fearless is falling madly in love again, even though you've been hurt before. Fearless is walking into your freshman year of high school at fifteen. Fearless is getting back up and fighting for what you want over and over again ... even though every time you've tried before, you've lost. It's Fearless to have faith that someday things will change. Fearless is having the courage to say goodbye to someone who only hurts you, even though can't breathe without them. I think it's Fearless to fall for your best friend, even though he's in love with someone else. And when someone apologizes to you enough times for things they'll never stop doing, I think it's Fearless to stop believing them. It's Fearless to say "you're NOT sorry". I think loving someone despite what people think is Fearless. I think allowing your-self to cry on the bathroom floor is Fearless. Letting go is Fearless. Then, moving on and being alright ... That's Fearless too. But no matter what love throws at you, you have to believe in it. You have to believe in love stories and prince charmings and happily ever after. That's why I write these songs. Because I think love is Fearless.

She had picked herself up after her romance with Joe Jonas, who was singled out in 'Forever and Always', and was evidently looking forward to finding love again.

Talking to About.comabout her title track, Taylor said: 'This is a song about the fearlessness of falling in love. No matter how many break-up songs you write, no matter how many times you get hurt, you will always fall in love again . . . I think sometimes when you're writing love songs you don't write them about what you're going through at that moment, you write them about what you wish you had.'

Other tracks included 'Fifteen', which Taylor said, 'was the best song she had ever written'. It chronicled her exploits with her best friend Abigail, who fell in love and was left heartbroken. She told CMT.com that it always made her very emotional when she sang it.

'That's a song about my best friend. I'm not likely to cry over something I've gone through, even if it's the worst break-up ever. Maybe I haven't had that break-up yet. Maybe there will be a break-up where I'll just cry every time I think of it. But the things that make me cry are when the people I love have gone through pain and I've seen it. 'Fifteen' talks about how my best friend, Abigail, got her heart broken when we were in ninth grade and singing about that absolutely gets me every time.'

Playful melody 'Hey Stephen' was a confessional number about her feelings for Stephen Barker of the country group Love and Theft.

She told the *New York Times*: 'This was a guy who opened

a couple of shows for me on tour. It was never anything like, he would know that I liked him. I don't ever confess that sort of thing in real life but I do like to confess it in my fantasy music life that I like to live. So I wrote this track called "Hey Stephen" and I sent Stephen a text message, that said, "Hey . . . Track five . . ."'

Another highlight was the understated ballad 'White Horse' – another bittersweet single about lost love.

'This girl falls in love with this guy and he's perfect,' she said. 'He's adorable. He's charming. He's endearing. She falls in love with him. Then she comes to realise he's leading a double life. He was already in a relationship a year before he even met her . . .'

The album was a phenomenal success, debuting at No. 1 on the *Billboard* 200 chart and selling almost 600,000 copies in the first week, the best opening sales for any female artist in 2008. It stayed in the top spot for eleven weeks – no other album had achieved that success in almost ten years.

The critics lapped it up and *Billboard* declared: 'Those who thought Taylor Swift was a big deal after the release of her first record be prepared: She's about to get way bigger. Though they're written by a teenager, Swift's songs have broad appeal, and therein lies the genius and accessibility in her second effort.'

Entertainment Weekly added: 'A button-cute blonde teen with a pocket full of hits – sounds like the early naughts all over again, no? But aside from sharing, possibly, a box of Clairol, there is nothing remotely Britney- or Christina-esque about Swift, the Pennsylvania-born country-pop wunderkind who conquered both Nashville and the mainstream with her 2006 debut.'

The *New York Times* said: 'Teenage subject matter notwithstanding, there's nothing naïve about this young singer's music; her second album is every bit as elegantly designed as her 2006 debut. Ms. Swift is one of pop's finest songwriters, country's foremost pragmatist and more in touch with her inner life than most adults.'

The *Boston Globe* said: 'Youth, it turns out, is the rising country star's greatest asset. But it's her knack for dissecting it so honestly that separates her from the pack of teenage starlets who rely on big-name producers, songwriters, and Disney shows for a music career. Swift is the rare ingenue who actually plays the part (and guitar). She's eighteen – wide-eyed, naive, hopeful – and that's how she sounds on *Fearless*, her superb new album out tomorrow on the indie label Big Machine Records.'

It later became the only album to spend a full year in the Top 10 on the *Billboard* 200, and became the second biggest-selling album in the last five years, behind Adele's *21*. Elsewhere, it also topped the charts in Canada and New Zealand and has sold more than 9 million copies across the world. It seemed to appeal to the younger teen generation with its angst-ridden songs about heartbreak and romance, just like a diary, and also to the older generation with its typical country-music arrangements and soft Southern twang.

Taylor was blown away by the response and later shared her delight with *Billboard*:

'It's really hard for me to wrap my mind around that one,'

she said about her chart success. 'In a business where longevity is what you aim for and hope for and strive for, having my album on the charts that long just absolutely floors me. That is such a long time. That's another one of those times where I've gotten a phone call and I really had to ask the person several times if they were serious and if they had really checked the math.'

She almost didn't have time to really let the huge significance of the numbers sink in because every producer on the biggest chat shows wanted Taylor on their sofa and her publicist Paula Erikson was bombarded with calls. She performed on *Good Morning America*, David Letterman's *Late Show* and *The Ellen DeGeneres Show*, where she sang 'Should've Said No' and 'Love Story', before being surprised on the sofa by Patrick Dempsey, from her favourite TV show, *Grey's Anatomy*, and Justin Timberlake, who she had admitted to the comedienne that she fancied. Later, she was interviewed by Jay Leno on *The Tonight Show* and performed 'White Horse'. She described the week of release, where she had many 4 a.m. wake-ups, as 'nuts'.

Andrea added: 'We both looked at each other and realized [Taylor] was living her dream.'

In the weeks that followed, it became clear she was now so famous that everyone wanted a piece of her. A 'Taylor Swift' doll for younger Swifties, complete with mini-Swarovski-crystal guitar, was released and Taylor even found herself duetting with one of her mother's favourite bands, Def Leppard, after TV channel CMT contacted her on behalf of their TV show, *Crossroads*, which paired up traditional country stars with bands from other genres. Taylor knew immediately that she would rock out alongside the hard metal group, who were also enthusiastic about the experiment.

Talking about the experience of singing a mixture of the two acts' songs, Taylor told *Time*: 'I was singing Def Leppard songs and they were singing my songs. It was just a complete out-of-body experience.' And the band's singer Joe Elliott reported: 'We brought the house down . . . Taylor is such a bundle of energy!'

Taylor was breaking boundaries and rules as she went, telling *Rolling Stone*: 'I'm inspired by all kinds of different sounds and I don't think I'd ever be someone who would say, "I will never make a song that sounds a certain way, I will never branch outside of genres," because I think that genres are sort of unnecessary walls.'

In November, she performed the single 'White Horse' at the American Music Awards (AMA) where she picked up the award for Favorite Country Music Female Artist in a gorgeous metallic dress.

'This is the first AMA I have ever won,' she squealed. 'The special thing about the American Music Awards is that they are voted on by the fans and also they are really shiny. I just want to thank all the wonderful people who went and bought my album this week and made it No. 1. It's an honour that you guys care so much about the songs I make up in my bedroom. You have no idea how much this means to me.'

She released her second single from the album, 'White

Horse', on 9 December, which marked a complete change in tack after 'Love Story'. The track had even featured in one of Taylor's favourite shows, *Grey's Anatomy*, back in September, which she described as a 'dream come true'.

She said: 'I actually wasn't going to put this song on the album. I was going to wait for the third album because I really felt like we had the "sadness" represented on this record. Then my agency out in LA set up a meeting with executive producers at *Grey's Anatomy* because that's my favourite show. It would just be a dream come true to have a song on it. So, I played them "White Horse".

'It was just me and my guitar and they freaked out. They loved it. They said, "We'll get back to you as soon as possible." For a while, we didn't know if we were going to put it on the record because if it wasn't going to be on the show, then we weren't going to put it on the album. Then they called and said they were very interested in the song. We recorded it right away, sent it off to them, and they put it in!'

She confessed: 'I've never been that excited. This is my life's goal, to have a song on *Grey's Anatomy*. My love of *Grey's Anatomy* has never wavered. It's my longest relationship to date!'

The video was a more sombre affair. Taylor noted: 'This video's a lot different than the other videos we've made because usually we've gone for bright colours and me looking straight into the camera and singing. But this one, it's a little more introspective. There's a pretty emotional scene in there where I had to cry for like three hours, like bawl my eyes out for three hours. It was really interesting and sort of a new thing for me.'

'White Horse' peaked at No. 13 in the *Billboard* Hot 100 and its appearance in the chart along with six other songs tied her with Miley Cyrus for the female act to have the most hits charting in the *Billboard* Hot 100 in the same week. Taylor was taking country music to a completely new level.

In January 2009, the country teen queen announced she would be fulfilling her long-held goal and embarking on her own headline Fearless tour, starting that April. With 105 shows across four countries in six months, she was going to have to work harder than ever before.

How she had time to tour is anyone's guess, between magazine covers, television appearances and award shows. As well as the hundreds of hours of preparation planning a gig that she had been fantasising about for years, she was the youngest country artist to make a guest appearance on the legendary TV show *Saturday Night Live*. Then, on the night of 9 February 2009, she attended the 51st Grammy Awards. While Taylor didn't receive any nominations, she sang her track 'Fifteen' with Miley Cyrus, who had dated Jonas brother Nick and broken up with him a few weeks before Taylor split with Joe.

The night before, she attended Clive Davis's pre-Grammy gala and was a bundle of nerves but admitted she felt relieved she would have Miley by her side.

'We're friends, so anytime I'm performing with her, my nerves go away, 'cause she's always trying to make me laugh or is doing something ridiculous,' she told MTV News. 'It's so fun to get up there with one of your friends and get to perform on the Grammys.'

That year, she also made a cameo appearance alongside Miley in *Hannah Montana: The Movie*, performing one of her songs in the background.

She told the *Today* show: 'Miley Cyrus is awesome. I love her so much. She is so incredibly sweet and funny.'

With two TV cameo appearances under her belt, Taylor was thrilled when she was offered her first proper acting job: a role in crime series *CSI*, another of her favourite shows.

'I've always joked around with my record label and my mum and everybody,' she told CBS. 'All my friends know it is my dream to die on *CSI*. I've always wanted to be one of the characters on there that they're trying to figure out what happened to.'

After hearing that she was a fan, the executive producer of the show arranged a meeting with Taylor. He offered her a part but told her it was one that she might not want as it didn't fit her pure image. It was that of Haley, a troubled and defiant teenager with a drug addict boyfriend – as the critics put it, 'the complete opposite of [Taylor] herself'.

However, Taylor relished the chance to play the part and she got her wish. When the show aired on 5 March, she was pictured lying dead in a car park and the mystery was solved through a series of flashbacks where her mouthy character was seen striking up a friendship with one of the detectives. In the end the audience learned that it was Haley's mother who killed her after accidentally stabbing her with a pair of scissors. Clearly, her fans had also tuned in because the episode gained more than 20 million viewers.

She wrote on MySpace: 'When I'm really old and can only remember one story about my life when I go back and relive and tell over and over again to the point when my grandchildren leave the room – that's the story. I got to guest on *CSI*!'

She received good reviews for her first proper role, with the *New York Times* noting 'pleasing flashes of subversion here, and a soft launch of her inevitable growing up, and out, of her porcelain persona.'

March 2009 marked another major step in Taylor's mission to conquer the wider showbiz scene: she graced the cover of *Rolling Stone*, introduced as: 'The biggest new pop star is a little bit country, a little bit rock & roll and all control freak,' with the headline: THE VERY PINK, VERY PERFECT LIFE OF TAYLOR SWIFT.

Taylor penned on her blog: 'I'm so excited, I can't even stand it. It's on the newsstands now, and I haven't seen it yet because I'm in London, but I can't believe I get to be on the cover of *Rolling Stone*. Wow. This is crazy.'

As well as admitting she had never smoked or drunk a drop of alcohol, when asked about her virginity after her relationship with Joe Jonas, she managed to sidestep the question and replied: 'I feel like whatever you say about whether you do or you don't, it makes people picture you naked. And as much as possible I'm going to avoid that.'

Taylor tried as best she could to avoid discussing her love life, keeping her replies centred on her music, which did the talking for her.

She seemed to be winning accolades at just about every pop and country awards show that existed. In April, she was invited to the Academy of Country Music Awards and was the youngest artist to ever receive the Album of the Year award for *Fearless*.

Her eyes glossed over with tears and she said: 'If you've ever talked to me for more than five minutes, then I'm going to write a song about you. I'd like to thank all the characters in my songs, Abigail, Tim McGraw, and Romeo!'

The same month, she won the ACM (Academy of Country Music Awards) best album award.

Her diary was planned down to the minute, such was the level of the work she had on. On 21 April, she also released her third single from the album, 'You Belong to Me', about one of her friend's relationships.

Taylor explained: 'I came into the writing session with Liz Rose and said, "I've got this idea." I had overheard a friend of mine talking to his girlfriend and he was completely on the defensive saying, "No, baby . . . I had to get off the phone really quickly . . . I tried to call you right back . . . Of course I love you. More than anything! Baby, I'm so sorry." She was just yelling at him! I felt so bad for him at that moment.' The story sees Taylor falling for him and writing about how she should've been the girl he was dating.

It was reviewed well, hailed as 'one of the best songs on *Fearless*', 'slick' and 'radio-friendly'. In the video, she portrays both the girlfriend (the popular girl) and the class geek (the narrator). These hints at her personal life were a revelation and the fans and press loved it.

Taylor had been dreaming of her first headline tour since she was a little girl and her fans were equally excited. There had been a huge rush for tickets, with the two nights at Los Angeles Staples Center selling out in two minutes and the gig at New York's historic Madison Square Garden selling out in a record of one minute.

The Fearless tour kicked off on 23 April in Indiana, which was named 'Taylor Swift Day' by the City Council president. Her choice of starting venue was a poignant and kooky one and typical of Taylor's decision-making.

'There was this group of girls when I was first starting out when I was sixteen years old, and I was playing the Wildhorse Saloon in Nashville,' she told a local TV station. 'The craziest group in the entire crowd was this group of twelve girls. So after the show, I told my mom, "You have got to get these girls." They were screaming and they made shirts and had their face paint on, like at a football game.'

The girls got to go backstage to meet Taylor and inspired the itinerary for her tour. She noted: 'They said they drove all the way there from Evansville, Indiana. So I've always had this really good vibe in my head when I thought of Evansville, because of these girls. So when they gave me options of where to start the tour, I was like, "That one!"'

The night before she started she was a bag of nerves,

checking every light cue and making sure everything would go off without a hitch. She wanted it to be faultless.

The theatrical and colourful 90-minute production certainly didn't disappoint. Set in three acts, it featured graphics, multiple costume changes, an illuminated castle and a spoof crime video showing all the guys who had inspired her songs complaining.

Taylor played five different guitars and the piano and veered from soft acoustic ballads to chair-flinging powerhouse rebellion. She worked the stage, flicking her hair, hugging fervent fans and squeezing outstretched hands and talking to her audience before each song, and was blown away by the reception she received. She loved her fans – every single one of them.

'Every single night I walk out on that stage, I'm always surprised by the roar of the crowd,' she said. 'That sound has always been a gift to me and never something I think I just deserve and never something that would just be given to me – I have to earn it.'

She has always been grateful for her unbelievable journey and revealed she had learned a lot from supporting other artists.

She said: 'I was able to open for some of the best acts in music for the last three years. I performed in the round with George Strait, in big stadiums with Kenny Chesney. It was educational to learn from the best talent out there, to be taking mental notes about stage configuration, how they ran their organisations – what I'd do different and what I'd emulate. I knew exactly how I wanted things to go.'

She invited other artists, including John Mayer, Faith Hill and Katy Perry, to perform one-off duets with her at various dates during the North American tour, while Justin Bieber, Kellie Pickler and Gloriana were the support acts. In the midst of her own tour, she even found the time and energy to open for Keith Urban on his Escape Together world tour.

A huge backing group of musicians, who had been with Taylor for three years, and dancers, who had won the job after open auditions, supported her and perfected their moves on tour 'boot camp'.

Talking about her band, she said: 'I couldn't live without them. They are my favorite people in the world.' Taylor often bought them presents and described them as 'her wonderful, loving family'. She was particularly close to Liz Huett, a backing singer, and Caitlin Evanson, her violinist, who she shared a dressing room with.

Andrea, who was always around as they travelled, was dubbed Momma Swift and found her role greeting people and drawing a 13 on Taylor's hand every night. Her dad, when he was there, would go around arenas handing out pictures of his daughter.

Taylor spent a lot of time hugging her fans after a 'cross arena trek' where she would pop up in a random part of the arena, play her song and then go out into the crowd. It was all part of making her audience feel special and part of the show.

'I hugged a lot of people over the course of that time,' she added in her DVD *Journey to Fearless*. 'I show a lot of extra love to the littler kids I know are there for a first concert. That's one of my favorite things. Every single night.'

She would give them her bracelets and make the 'worst' seats in the house the best ones for part of the performance.

'Every night, the crowd gave so much and I wanted to give them something back,' she said.

During the tour, her mum loved to run backstage tours for her army of fans and would search the crowd during concerts to pick out the biggest fan to award them with the dream of a lifetime: Taylor Swift Tea Party – or 'T-Party' – passes to go backstage and meet her after the concert in a Moroccan-inspired tent, where they would play ping-pong and relax. 'It's a way for me to get to meet people after the show who I fell in love with after the concert and who I just feel grateful to have by my side,' she explained.

Her fans – both men and women – couldn't get enough of Taylor. They painted their faces, waved banners and screamed her name. Taylor showed them how much she cared for them by holding up her hand in a heart shape – known as the 'hand heart', and flashed by other stars such as Justin Bieber, Selena Gomez, Demi Lovato and Blake Lively.

'The heart-hand symbol means something between "I love you" and "thank you", Taylor said. 'It's just a sweet, simple message that you can deliver without saying a word.'

In June, Taylor attended the CMT Awards and sparkled in a Collette Dinnigan dress, paired with strappy Prada heels. She also had a very special date for the night, her brother

Austin. She tweeted: 'I finally convinced my brother to go to an award-show with me. Ground-breaking.'

For the second year on the trot, she claimed Best Video and Best Female Video, both for 'Love Story'.

She often singled out her fans above anyone else and told the crowd: 'Thank you to the fans that come out to my shows and spend such hard work making these amazing scrapbooks and writing me letters. Reading your letters and reading your MySpace comments, anytime I have a bad day, you make those days good.'

Taylor also had the audience in fits of laughter when the show opened with a spoof video, *Thug Story*, where she laughed at herself when T-Swift and T-Pain made fun of her clean-living image, with lyrics like, 'I knit sweaters, yo,' and 'I'm a gangsta you can find me baking cookies at night.'

Taylor-mania was starting to seep across into international waters and as part of her tour she played some UK dates at the Shepherd's Bush Empire and was quickly embraced by the British public.

The *Guardian* said: 'Her regulation blonde bounciness and bubbly ditties about high-school Romeos make her deceptively similar to the likes of Miley Cyrus – there is also a matter of her gushing about our "adorable accents" – it seems Swift really cares what she is doing.'

Taylor went back to the USA before returning to the UK to play the V Festival in August, where she performed five of her top hits before popping into Radio 1 and doing a string of interviews.

Then she gigged again at Wembley Arena, and the

Manchester Evening News (MEN) Arena, in November. Justin Bieber was her support act, but while singing at Wembley he broke his foot when he tripped over in the opening lines of his hit, 'One Time'. He continued to sing, but missed his encore so he could be rushed to hospital for an X-ray.

The following night, in Manchester, the audience went crazy as he managed his set and encore and Taylor told them: 'Every time I hear the word Manchester, I won't be able to stop smiling . . . I love you!'

She loved touring Europe and visiting countries she had never been to before and embraced every second of her unbelievable journey.

While she was on tour, she released 'Fifteen', and it was yet another commercial success, peaking at No. 21 in the *Billboard* Hot 100 and selling over 1 million downloads in the USA. The critics loved its personal approach and felt it was a standout track on the album. During her concerts, she performed a stripped-back version of the track while sitting on a wooden stool with her 12-string.

The Fearless tour was still going strong. It was charming her packed audiences and had critics falling over themselves.

Reuters said: 'The key selling point on display was Swift's relatability. She's not just another oversexed, underdressed prefab pop Barbie, but rather the girl next door who's had her heart broken and takes refuge in music she actually sings, plays and writes . . . She has a likable stage presence that's not overly polished and even was slightly awkward at times.'

The *Los Angeles Times* added: 'Her fans don't just believe in her savvy songwriting and gracious, magnetic stage presence. They trust her as a peer . . . When she stood beneath a cascading waterfall to close her encore, she looked every bit the pop star, but also every bit a teenager – drenched, giddy and with a bit of explaining to do when she gets home past curfew.'

Taylor was delighted with the reaction. She was on a roll: the media loved her, her fan base was multiplying by the day and 2009 was becoming even more successful than her breakthrough year of 2008. And while it seemed that nothing could go wrong for the starlet, just around the corner was one of the biggest music furores of 2009. And Taylor was right at the centre of it.

CHAPTER SIX

'You know I'm not gonna say that I wasn't rattled by it'

The MTV Video Music Awards (VMAs) is one of the biggest and starriest nights in the showbiz calendar. Dubbed the 'Oscars for Youth', it is more hip than the Grammys and far more influential than the many country award ceremonies that Taylor had previously attended. Since Madonna burst on to the stage at the inaugural event in 1984, wearing a combination of a bustier and wedding dress, to perform 'Like a Virgin', the awards have always courted the headlines for their outrageous antics.

The star-studded 2009 event at Radio City Music Hall in New York was a big deal for Taylor, who was nominated for the Best Female Video award for her single, 'You Belong to Me'. The host, Russell Brand, had sparked controversy the previous year by making a quip about the Jonas Brothers' chastity pledge, so the audience knew they were in for another night of cutting commentary.

After a tribute to Michael Jackson, Taylor was presented with the award for the first category of the night, Best Female Video, by Taylor Lautner and Shakira. The songstress had beaten off stiff competition from her rivals including Beyoncé, who was up for her video for 'Single Ladies (Put a Ring on It)', Lady Gaga for 'Poker Face' and Pink for 'So What'.

Taylor, who was dressed in a KaufmanFranco dress adorned with sequins, was ecstatic to win her first VMA gong, dubbed a Moonman. By then, she was fairly well practised at acceptance speeches and always won the audience over with her down-to-earth charm and genuine awe. It was her moment to shine.

Then something happened that evoked sympathy and outrage on her behalf. As 27 million homes watched the events unfold, Kanye West jumped on the stage from where he was sitting in the audience and interrupted a nervous Taylor, who had started saying: 'I always wondered what it would be like to maybe win one of these some day, but never actually thought it would happen . . .'

The R&B star, who had reportedly been seen swigging Hennessy Cognac on the red carpet earlier in the night, proceeded to grab the microphone and told a visibly stunned audience: 'Yo, Tay, I'm really happy for you and I'm gonna let you finish but Beyoncé had one of the best videos of all time. One of the best videos of all time!' Taylor's face fell and the cameras panned round to a horrified-looking

Beyoncé. Taylor glanced down at the floor and mouthed 'What?' and began to walk away, looking wounded. Kanye was booed loudly before he stormed off backstage.

Chief Executive Officer of Rap Radar, Elliott Wilson, who was sitting near Kanye in the vast auditorium, told CNN: 'At first, people weren't sure if it was kind of like a gag. You could feel everybody being nervous and not knowing if it was a prank or something. Then people started booing him really loud. The reaction to his tantrum was so strong . . . and what happened was he gave everyone the finger.'

Just a few moments later, Taylor was ushered through the VIP exit to begin a rendition of 'You Belong with Me' outside the venue in a subway station and then on the front of a yellow cab. Ever the consummate professional, she persevered and gave a convincing performance but, back in the privacy of her dressing room, she burst into tears and was comforted by Beyoncé's father and manager, Matthew Knowles. Taylor's mum, Andrea, who was outraged, approached Kanye to dress him down but he just shrugged and repeated that he thought Beyoncé's video was better.

A video of the incident immediately went viral and was eventually seen 2 million times on the MTV website alone.

Taylor was distraught but knew she had to get through the evening, so joined other guests in the auditorium. Later, Beyoncé showed grace and class when she invited Taylor on stage when she won an award for 'Single Ladies (Put a Ring on It)' in the Video of the Year. First, Beyoncé told the audience about her first VMA win as a 17-year-old, with Destiny's Child, and how much it had meant to her and, then, she sportingly brought the teen singer back on stage to huge applause. The pair, both dressed in bright red, hugged before Beyoncé passed the microphone to the Taylor, who said: 'Maybe we could try this again,' to a standing ovation from the audience.

'I would really like to thank Roman White, who directed the video, and Lucas Till for being in it,' she said. 'I would like to thank all the fans on Twitter and MySpace and everyone that came out to my shows this summer. And I would like to thank my little brother's high school for letting us shoot there.'

She had succeeded in keeping her head held high. Kanye was ejected from the event and, after some stern words from his management team, no doubt, he quickly issued a statement on his blog:

I'M SOOOOO SORRY TO TAYLOR SWIFT AND HER FANS AND HER MOM,' HE WROTE. 'I SPOKE TO HER MOTHER RIGHT AFTER AND SHE SAID THE SAME THING MY MOTHER WOULD'VE SAID. SHE IS VERY TALENTED! I LIKE THE LYRICS ABOUT BEING A CHEER-LEADER AND SHE'S IN THE BLEACHERS! . . . .
I'M IN THE WRONG FOR GOING ON STAGE AND TAKING AWAY FROM HER MOMENT! . . . . BEYONCÉ'S VIDEO WAS THE BEST OF THIS DECADE!!!! I'M SORRY TO MY FANS IF I LET YOU GUYS DOWN!!!! I'M SORRY TO MY FRIENDS AT MTV. I WILL APOLOGIZE TO TAYLOR 2MRW. WELCOME TO THE REAL WORLD!!!! EVERYBODY WANNA BOOOOO ME BUT I'M A FAN OF REAL POP CULTURE!!! NO DISRESPECT BUT WE WATCHIN' THE SHOW AT THE CRIB RIGHT NOW CAUSE . . . WELL YOU KNOW!!!! I'M STILL HAPPY FOR TAYLOR!!!! BOOOYAAAWWWW!!!! YOU ARE

VERY VERY TALENTED!!! I GAVE MY AWARDS TO OUTKAST
WHEN THEY DESERVED IT OVER ME ... THAT'S WHAT IT IS!!!!!!!
I'M NOT CRAZY YALL, I'M JUST REAL. SORRY FOR THAT!!! I
REALLY FEEL BAD FOR TAYLOR AND I'M SINCERELY SORRY!!!
MUCH RESPECT!!!!!

It wasn't the first time Kanye had an angry rant during an awards ceremony. At the American Music Awards in 2004, he stormed out after losing the Best New Artist gong, saying: 'I was definitely robbed ... I was the best new artist this year.' In 2006, when his single 'Touch the Sky' failed to win Best Video at the European Music Awards, he went on stage and argued that he should have won instead.

The following year, he suggested that his race had something to do with being overlooked for the opening act at the MTV VMAs in favour of Britney Spears. He got angry after it was revealed that his performance would take place in a hotel room rather than the event's main stage and, after failing to win any of the five awards he was nominated for, he claimed he would never return to MTV.

It seems the public had had enough of Kanye's tantrums and his apology wasn't nearly enough.

Pink, who had to be escorted away from Kanye inside the auditorium, tweeted: 'Kanye West is the biggest piece of s*** on earth. Quote me. My heart goes out to Taylor Swift. She is a sweet and talented girl and deserved her moment. She should know we all love her. Beyoncé is a classy lady. I feel for her, too. It's not her fault at all, and her and Taylor did their thing. And douche bag got kicked out.'

Katy Perry wrote: 'F*** you Kanye. It's like you stepped on a kitten,' while Kelly Clarkson added on her blog: 'What happened to you as a child? Did you not get hugged enough?'

And Good Charlotte singer Joel Madden added: 'WOW, Taylor Swift's first VMA and she didn't even get to ENJOY it! Kanye you were a bully on that one man.'

As a social media hurricane ensued, Taylor told reporters after the event that she had been getting many messages of support and that she felt indebted to Beyoncé for giving up her moment to allow her to speak.

'It was just so wonderful and so incredibly classy of her and just gracious and wonderful to let me say something. She's just been my hero and one of my idols ever since I was little. Before the talented artist, the superstar, she's always been a great person and I just, I thought I couldn't love Beyoncé more tonight, than tonight.'

In a twist that no one would have imagined, the following day, US President Barack Obama was asked by CNBC during an interview if his daughters were upset by what had happened to Taylor.

He replied: 'I thought that was really inappropriate. You know it was like, she was getting an award and what are you butting in? [. . .] The young lady seems like a perfectly nice person, she's getting her award and what's he doing up there? He's a jackass.'

A media frenzy ensued, with everyone talking about what had happened during 'KanyeGate' and the artist appeared on *The Jay Leno Show* to try to attempt some damage control, blaming his antics on the death of his mother, Donda, who had passed away after complications from cosmetic surgery in 2007.

He said: 'It's been extremely difficult, just dealing with the fact that I hurt someone or took anything away, you know, from a talented artist – or from anyone. But I need to, after this, take some time off and just analyse how I'm going to make it through the rest of this life, how I'm going to improve. Because I am a celebrity, and that's something I have to deal with. It was rude, period. And, you know, I'd like to be able to apologize to her in person. And I wanted to . . .'

Two days afterwards, Taylor also had her say when she appeared on the popular daytime TV show, *The View*. Naturally, the singer was asked about it while she sat on the sofa, and she revealed she was 'rattled' by the event.

'Well, I think my overall thought process was something like, "Wow, I can't believe I won, this is awesome, don't trip or fall. I'm gonna get to thank the fans, this is so cool. Oh, Kanye West is here. Cool haircut. What are you doing here?" And then, "Ouch." And then, "I guess I'm not gonna get to thank the fans."'

She continued: 'You know I'm not gonna say that I wasn't rattled by it, but I had to perform five minutes later, so I had to get myself back to a place where I could perform.'

According to the shows' publicists, Kanye picked up the phone and personally expressed his regret to Taylor, who accepted his apologies.

She told ABC News Radio: 'He was very sincere in his apology and I accepted that apology.'

She refused to be drawn in to what had been said during the exchange and was desperate to put the unhappy event behind her.

'I'm just honestly trying not to make it into a bigger deal than it already is,' she told the *MJ Morning Show*. 'It's become more of a big deal than I ever thought it would be. It happened on TV, so everybody saw what happened. I would just like to move on.'

However, the impact of what had happened was immense – overnight, Taylor became a household name across the globe. Even Scott Borchetta revealed on National Public Radio that the incident 'did end up being positive in her career in terms of name recognition'.

Taylor also said that in her typical fashion she wouldn't let it detract from the good run she had been having.

'I've had a few days – and everyone has them – when you feel humiliated or you're shocked by something or something knocks you down a few pegs. But in those moments, I've been very quick to realise and remind myself that there are people out there with real problems. To get hung up on any bad moment that happened this year would be unfair to all the good moments I've had this year.'

However, it seems like Kanye's apology might have been empty, as the following year he made three separate digs at her. During an interview on New York's Hot 97 radio station, he first argued that what he had said was not wrong, just that he had timed it badly, saying: 'I made a mistake. My timing was definitely extremely off and the bigger plans, the bigger fight – how do you go about it? How do you go about getting it done?'

Bizarrely, he said he felt like Taylor should defend him more widely, not just when people asked her about the incident.

'She just talked about how, you know, people would come up to her in the grocery store and really just bring it up, and she would defend me at the grocery store – I'm sorry, defend me in an interview, she said at her grocery store, she was actually defending me. It's an amazing, compelling situation.'

He then went on to argue that far from being a selfish act, his intention was just the opposite, as he wanted to see Beyoncé appreciated.

'What was arrogant about that?' He asserted: 'That's completely selfless. That's like jumping in front of a bullet. I lost an arm. I'm walking around, I'm trying to put my album out with one arm right now. Every time I try to perform a song, everybody's like, well, what's up with that missing arm, though?'

As the debate continued to roar, Taylor's diary was packed with more awards ceremonies; maybe Kanye didn't rate her music but clearly the rest of the music world did.

In November, she graced the red carpet in a floor-length Reem Acra gown at her second CMA Awards show where she was up for four categories including the most prized country music award, Entertainer of the Year. She would face Kenny Chesney, who had won it four of the previous five years.

After opening the proceedings with a rousing performance of 'Forever and Always', in which she threw a chair off the podium and slid down a pole, she began to sweep the board, as she picked up Music Video of the Year for 'Love Story', Album of the Year for *Fearless* and, then, when she was announced as the winner of Female Vocalist of the Year, she poked fun at the rap star and said: 'I want to thank every single person here for not running up on to stage during my speech.'

Hosts Carrie Underwood and Brad Paisley also took a few swipes at Kanye, with a parody of 'Mamas, don't let your babies grow up to be cowboys', reworked to 'Mamas, don't let your babies grow up to be Kanye'. There was also some banter about Brad's 'Welcome to the Future' video, when 88-year-old veteran star Little Jimmy Dickens crashed the stage and interrupted the pair.

'Excuse me, sir,' he said, cutting Brad off. 'I'll let you finish later. I know you had a nice video and all, but Taylor Swift made the best video of all time. Of all time! You go, girl!' The cameras cut to Taylor, who, along with the crowd, was laughing at the gag.

Finally, Taylor picked up the best prize of all – Entertainer of the Year – and was handed her gong by her favourite country couple, Faith Hill and Tim McGraw. As her name was announced, the audience at the Sommet Center in Nashville went berserk, with teenagers and fans shouting her name.

She said: 'I'll never forget this moment because in this moment everything that I could ever wanted has just happened to me. You guys, this album is my diary, and so to all the people who voted for me for this . . . thank you for saying you love my diary because that's the nicest compliment.'

The critics were quick to ask whether this kind of success had come too soon, but Taylor confidently hit back: 'I feel like it has been fast but it's also been a growth curve. I've watched the CMA Awards for as long as I can remember, and I got to come to my first one when I was fifteen. I know what it means to win a CMA award. So I look at it from both ways.'

The next month, she had another blinding set of wins at the American Music Awards, having most nominations along with Michael Jackson, who had died four months earlier, picking up five gongs and beating the King of Pop to the Favourite Pop/Rock Artist of the Year. She wasn't able to attend the event as she was in London, but gratefully accepted them via video link from backstage at Wembley Arena.

'Music has never been ultimately about competition,' she said, adding that it was an 'unimaginable honor' to be cited in the same category as Michael Jackson, and thanked his family.

By this point, Taylor was never out of the headlines for long and as the weeks wore on, she was in the spotlight yet again – this time because of her rumoured new boyfriend. Sharing the same name, successful careers and good looks, Taylor and her new man Taylor Lautner seemed like the perfect union.

They had met on the set of *Valentine's Day*, Taylor's feature-film debut about a series of couples that make up and break up on Valentine's Day, featuring a star-studded ensemble cast, including Jessica Alba, Jamie Foxx, Bradley Cooper, Anne Hathaway and Jennifer Garner. Taylor was very busy when she was approached about the flick but loved the romantic theme, and Hollywood veteran Garry Marshall, who directed *Pretty Woman* and *Runaway Bride*, was at the helm.

'I got a phone call from Garry Marshall,' she told Trailer Addict.com, 'saying, "Taylor, I want to have lunch or breakfast with you. I really want you to be in this movie. Will you? Will you let me write a part for you?" And I could not believe it. I couldn't believe it, because I didn't have the time to be a big role in this movie, Garry was going to write a small part for me. It blew my mind.'

Taylor was cast as Felicia, a sweet and innocent teen opposite Taylor Lautner, as her boyfriend, Willy. The affair saw them agreeing to wait until Valentine's Day to consummate their relationship and they had been filming in a high school.

'We're walking in school and it's interesting because we shot this scene in an active high school,' Taylor laughed during a press conference. 'Active. As in school is in session while we're filming. Every thirty minutes, there would be a bell that would ring and hundreds of students were pouring out, exactly where we were, and there were loads of people screaming out of windows and groups of kids gathering together chanting things. It was definitely an interesting and very exciting day, For me to step out of my comfort zone and try comedy, and have one of the coolest directors and legendary director laughing that hard at my first scene, it was really wonderful.'

Taylor had to kiss the actor who, at seventeen, was two years her junior and had risen to fame playing the werewolf Jacob in the *Twilight* series. Afterwards, she admitted she enjoyed the embrace, jokingly calling it 'life-changing'.

'I love him, he's so cute,' she gushed, and he revealed he fancied her, declaring she was definitely 'his type'.

'We got along great,' he told *Rolling Stone*. 'We instantly clicked. And she's – she's an amazing girl. Aside from being beautiful, she's extremely funny, charismatic and fun to be around, and so we definitely get along. We're close.'

The pair were first seen side by side watching a basketball match at the end of October and a few days later enjoyed a romantic dinner at the Ruth's Chris Steak House in Beverly Hills. The singer played it cool and when she was asked about the romance on CMT Radio, she coyly replied: 'I don't know, he's an amazing guy and we're really close and . . . ah yep . . . and we're in a movie together and I'm really excited about seeing it.'

The new couple – nicknamed Tay Tay by the media – were instant tabloid fodder with magazines and newspapers following their every move. The actor was noted watching two of Taylor's concerts in Chicago and another date at a hockey game followed. Afterwards they were seen in the lobby of the Beverly Wilshire Hotel and later on more dates, chaperoned by Andrea.

People magazine declared: 'Taylor Swift was all dolled up and looked super pretty. She didn't seem to mind the attention. Taylor Lautner, on the other hand, was hiding under a hoodie.'

Taylor with straightened hair, long before she was famous

The nervous-looking singer poses for photographers at her first ever awards show in 2006

Hugging her favourite guitar, not long after the release of her eponymous debut album

With close friend Kellie Pickler at the Academy of Country Music (ACM) Awards, where Taylor finally got to meet the man who inspired her first single

Dressed to impress, Taylor arrives at the CMAs in November 2007

She wows the crowd at the Academy of Country Music Awards by performing 'Should've Said No' under falling rain

With rumoured boyfriend Joe Jonas at the MTV Video Music Awards

The infamous moment at the VMAs when Kanye West stormed the stage in September 2009

Singing alongside John Mayer at Z100's Jingle Ball, months before rumours that the pair were dating began to circulate

Showing off an edgier look at the
American Music Awards in 2010

Taylor poses with her six
Grammys, including the Album
of the Year gong for *Fearless*

Gleefully crowd surfing at the Academy of Country Music Awards

Taylor poses with president and CEO of Big Machine Records, Scott Borchetta

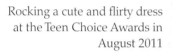

Rocking a cute and flirty dress at the Teen Choice Awards in August 2011

Taylor describes her good friend Selena Gomez as a 'little sister'

The singer is overwhelmed when she is presented with the Nickelodeon Kids' Choice Big Help Award for her charity work by Michelle Obama

Reaching for the sea of hands during her performance of 'We Are Never Ever Getting Back Together' at the 2012 VMAs

Singing alongside her good pal, co-writer and *Red* tour support act Ed Sheeran at the Z100 Jingle Ball

With her devoted parents, Andrea and Scott, who have always believed in Taylor's ability

Haylor spend a romantic afternoon together in New York's Central Park in December 2012

During an energetic and raunchy routine of 'I Knew You Were Trouble' at the BRIT Awards in London

Harry and Taylor chat to fans at a tattoo shop in LA where Harry was getting a new inking on his arm

Taylor tries to put ex-boyfriend Harry out of her mind as she poses on the red carpet at the BRIT Awards

During a fun and colourful rendition of '22' at the Billboard Music Awards

On the road with her *Red* tour, the young star plays to a stadium crowd of more than 48,000 fans

Taylor scoops an incredible eight accolades at the Billboard Music Awards and thanks her fans, saying: 'You are the longest and best relationship I have ever had'

Performing the role of the ringmaster during 'We Are Never Ever Getting Back Together' on her sold-out *Red* tour

Lautner then hinted at the relationship, telling a magazine: 'The very funny thing is that all of you have seen every single move I make, so I guess I can leave that up to you to decide.'

In November, Taylor guest-hosted the iconic show *Saturday Night Live* (*SNL*) and was just the twelfth person in thirty-five years to be asked to perform the honours. She wrote her opening monologue and it seemed like a good time to poke fun at herself, referencing her break-up with Joe and the Kanye West incident. She also hinted at her new romance.

The show went down a storm, with *Entertainment Weekly* calling Taylor 'the season's best host so far'.

They declared: 'Whether shrewdly letting her Kate Gosselin wig do most of the acting during a typically pungent parody of *The View*, or gleefully screeching while wearing braces in a public-service commercial satirizing texting-while-driving, Swift was always up for the challenge, seemed to be having fun, and helped the rest of the cast nail the punchlines.'

Taylor seemed to be breaking out of her whiter-than-white cast and showing more of the fun side of her personality and the audience loved her for it. Her humour made her accessible to the millions of viewers who regularly tuned in and the lady herself declared it was 'the best week of my life'.

'I started as a theatre kid so *SNL* has been on a pedestal for me and I've always wondered what it would be like to actually experience it. You don't even notice you're so busy you have to eat while you're walking to your next meeting. I was at 30 Rock at 7 a.m. until one or two at night a lot of times. I didn't want to leave. I was definitely stepping out of my comfort zone in terms of how people have seen me in the past. To see the reviews come in and them be positive and the ratings come in and the fans were so wonderful and made a point to watch, it made me so thankful and so happy.'

A month later, Taylor Lautner hosted the show and got his revenge on Kanye for embarrassing his girlfriend, in a skit. It started by showing the clip of the moment he stole Taylor's thunder.

'I was actually on stage with her when that happened – as you can see I really stood up for her,' he joked, as the clip showed him looking around awkwardly. At that point, he was shown to be standing beside two dummies, one dressed like Taylor, the other Kanye. He went through a dazzling martial arts routine of flips and kicks – ending by him knocking Kanye's head off. He then went in for a kiss with the pretend Swift before pulling away, saying he was in love with another – the camera turning to a man in drag pretending to be country star Reba McEntire.

The only downside of Taylor's ever-increasing fame was the attention from paparazzi and media. She was mobbed wherever she went and popping out to the shops to pick up a pint of milk or going out for a meal was almost impossible but she said it never bothered her.

'There's going to be a line that forms in front of the table and I'm going to be signing autographs the entire time,' she told the *Daily Mail*. 'I can't look at that as a burden, because that's what I've always wanted.'

The songstress had always maintained that she tried to lead a normal life where she could, telling MTV's *The Seven*: 'I'm very conscious of the path that I chose in life and this it is a different path than what my friends chose. College and living in a dorm, that would've been my life. I always keep one eye on that path ... I have no regrets about the path that I took, but I still try to experience as much as I possibly can in life. Loving this is part of my life and sometimes, if you get too tired or you're jetlagged, you might forget. But I always remind myself I love this.'

While she had been going to awards ceremonies, giving interviews and dating, she had also been continuing on her Fearless tour, which wound up towards the end of 2009. Taylor was delighted with how it had gone.

'Every night feels like a celebration,' she said. 'I never expected it to be as successful as it was.'

As her final night wrapped, Taylor said it was 'really sad' and described it as being like 'impending graduation'. After the final show, she gave her team a 'yearbook'.

Her production had eventually played to more than 1.1 million fans and the box office tills rang up an astonishing $63 million. She was on the road for fifteen months, 'looping around the world' from America to the UK, Canada, Australia and Japan.

'It's the coolest thing in the world,' she said in *Journey to Fearless*. 'I mean, that's just something you fantasize and dream about, not something that really happens, is it? It had heart ...

'This tour ending is very symbolic of more than just a

tour ending . . . it's like the entire Fearless era of my life is ending. It's been a long time on this particular project . . . It's been a beautiful, beautiful time with the word Fearless being at the forefront of my life and career. That project and album has gone further than I ever imagined it could.'

Her father, Scott, summed up: 'When you think about where it started and how much she loves singing and how much she loves her fans, and everything else. What a way to end the year.'

As soon as the run of dates ended, Taylor was back holed up in the recording studio in Nashville, although much of the material was already under her belt.

She said: 'I actually am best writing on the road. I only have time to write songs that hit me the hardest. Those are songs like 'Fifteen' – that's one I wrote on the road. It hit me and I needed to write it so I found time to write it, whether it's fifteen minutes between a meet-and-greet or at 4 a.m. If they haunt me throughout my meet-and-greets and interviews and all I'm playing in my head, then I know I've got something. I'm well into writing my next album. I think my biggest goal for this next record is to write in real time as I always have.'

However, things with Taylor Lautner were going less smoothly and by the singer's twentieth-birthday party on 13 December, their relationship was over.

A source told *Us Weekly* magazine: 'There was no chemistry and it felt contrived . . . He liked her more than she liked him. He went everywhere he could to see her, but she didn't travel much to see him. They plan to stay friends.'

Before the release of *Valentine's Day*, Taylor was interviewed in *Girls' Life* magazine and spoke about having rules for love – including, 'love your single status', 'take all kinds of compliments', 'look for love everywhere', 'put your friends before your fellas' and 'be yourself!' among others.

One of her main points was 'break-ups happen for a reason'. She wrote: 'However hard and painful they are, you will learn something from a break-up. That is the most contrived, you've-heard-it-a-million-times lesson, but I really do feel like everything is put in your life to teach you something – even if it is terrible or hard.'

Naturally, she wrote about what she had learned and 'Back to December' was an apology for being the heartbreaker this time round.

'It's an apology in the form of a song,' she said in TV show, *Taylor Swift: Speak Now*. 'You know, in life, you learn lessons. And sometimes you learn them the hard way. Sometimes you learn them too late. The song "Back to December" is about a lesson I learned too late. And I think, when you do that, and you finally realise that you were wrong, you need to say you're sorry. And this was the best way that I knew how.'

Taylor believed that when she found the right man for her, she would know.

She told *Girls' Life*: 'It's funny, you can know a guy for a year and never feel like they truly know you. Then you meet someone else, and within the first five minutes of conversation, you feel like they truly understand who you are. I'm all about finding that connection.'

She spent the Christmas and the New Year at home with her family and friends celebrating her success.

'I was back in Nashville, and it was pretty cool – my brother's leaving for college next year and I'm moving out in a few months, so this was sort of a moment in time for me,' she told *Rolling Stone*. 'I was definitely recording all of it in my mind, the last Christmas with us being in the same place.'

Around this time, she also bought her first home by herself, an airy 4,000-square-foot penthouse at the Adelicia, a newly constructed, fully serviced building in downtown Nashville, for $2 million. According to reports, her new pad was decorated in a 'whimsical, quirky, eclectic treehouse-style'.

Taylor, who is a big fan of interior design, said: 'You step on a stepping stone in the pond in order to get on a spiral staircase, which takes you up to the human-sized birdcage observatory. They're delivering a human-sized birdcage, which I'll put a brass telescope in. The ceiling of my living room is painted like the night sky.'

Other highlights included a moat-surrounded fireplace filled with koi carp. She told the *New Yorker*: 'I was obsessive about turning my apartment into an art project.'

She styled two of her rooms on her friends. 'The two guest rooms are inspired by my two best friends in Nashville. One is Caitlin, my fiddle player; she's very earthy.

So "her" room has a quilt on the bed,' she explained to *Glamour* magazine. 'Liz, my other best friend, is very trendy and kind of princess-y, so in her room, there's a French Victorian-looking silver bed. I had so much fun with it. The condo is at the top of a building and very modern, but it feels like a pirate ship . . . Everything is mismatched: the pillows, the fabrics, the paintings, the dishes. That takes the pressure off me – it means *I* don't have to match.'

Due to the intense nature of being on the road, Taylor welcomed the time alone and the freedom to have her friends over.

'I love living alone,' she said. 'When all my friends went off to college when I was eighteen, I was on tour, so I never really had time to move out. It's so much fun having my independence and so much space, having friends over whenever I want and cooking all the time. All of a sudden I care about keeping it clean because it's my house.'

She explained that she still saw her mum a lot and was very rarely on her own.

'I've always been independent, but I still see my mom a lot. And since I've been working solidly every single day since I've moved in, I've never spent a day alone in the place. When I get home [at night], there's that quiet. Except for the sound of trickling water in the pond and fountain.'

On New Year's Eve 2009, she returned to her family home after going out for dinner.

'It was a low-key night. I went to dinner with my friend Hayley [Williams, from the band Paramore] and drove home, where my brother was having a party. I was hiding in my room listening to the dynamics of a senior-class party. There was the loud girl screaming that it was her birthday like 400 times, then there was drama when a kid got pushed into the lake and almost got hypothermia.

'I was texting Hayley to let her know I got home from dinner, and that my paranoid thoughts of getting in a car wreck were unwarranted. So I think I texted her something like, "Don't worry about me, I'm not dead," and I looked at the clock and it was midnight. So I actually got to experience looking at the clock when it struck midnight, and that was a really fun moment for me, it was the most unconventional New Year's Eve I've ever had.'

It was a welcome glimpse of normality for the star. The year 2009 had been a blinding one for Taylor. *Forbes* ranked her as the year's 69th most powerful celebrity, earning a staggering $18 million, and *Billboard* named her their Artist of the Year.

They summed up: 'She's sold more albums than any artist not named Michael Jackson. Her first headlining tour, Fearless 2009, sold out every show within minutes. She became the youngest woman to win the Country Music Association's Entertainer of the Year award and she set seemingly every chart record that exists.'

The Kanye West incident aside, everything Taylor touched seemed to turn to gold.

CHAPTER SEVEN

'I think it's the writer in me that's a little more obsessed with the meaning of the song than the vocal technique'

It seemed that whatever Taylor put her mind to she could conquer. She had seen the good, the bad and the ugly of the industry and she had survived. No doubt she was hoping that 2010 would build on the phenomenal success of 2009.

However, somewhat inevitably, a Taylor Swift backlash started to mushroom as her fame increased. Like any highly ruthless industry, the flip side of the coin is there will always be a certain amount of backbiting about the artists who have made it by the ones who continue to flounder when success proves elusive. Within Nashville's bars, recording studios, restaurants and offices were singers hoping for a bite of the cherry who had been pushing for fame a lot longer than Taylor. They said she was a sugar-coated Barbie who didn't really write her own songs, that she had just been lucky and had a wealthy father who had bought her success.

Taylor ignored the rumours and whispers and set about releasing her first single of the year, the fifth and final single, 'fearless' from the album of the same name, on 4 January: another hit, 'Today Was a Fairytale', which was released on 22 January and featured on the soundtrack to the film *Valentine's Day*. It was an old track that she had written in 2008, but Taylor said she went back to it.

'When this movie opportunity came about, I reached back into my pocket and thought, "I think this is perfect for the soundtrack. I hope it's perfect for the soundtrack,"' she explained to the *Tennessean*.

It debuted at No. 2 on the *Billboard* Hot 100 and sold 325,000 digital copies in the first week – breaking the record for first week download sales by a female artist, previously set by Britney Spears for 'Womanizer'.

Even bigger success would follow. In December, she had found out that she had a staggering eight nominations for the Grammy Awards, three more than pop star Lady Gaga. She was in a hotel room with her mum editing a home video for her website when the news came through and she screamed when she heard her name.

She told Associated Press (AP): 'To be recognized by the Grammys is the ultimate honour, and all I know is that when I write about this in my journal tonight it will all be capital letters and underlined four times, and there will be lots of exclamation points in this entry because I never imagined I'd get to write this kind of journal entry.'

The singer joined a star-studded crowd on 31 January at the Staples Center in Los Angeles, and wowed on the red carpet in a Kaufman Franco gown and elaborate jewellery. Leading the pack was Beyoncé, who picked up six Grammys out of an overall ten nominations. Amazingly, Taylor took four, including Best Country Album, and Best Country Song and Best Female Country Vocal Performance for 'White Horse'. She also became the youngest artist in history to pick up Album of the Year for *Fearless*, beating the likes of pop A-listers Beyoncé, Lady Gaga, Dave Matthews and the Black Eyed Peas. It was a monumental achievement.

'I hope you know how much this means to me and all my producers that we can take this back to Nashville,' she said. 'This is the story that when we're eighty years old and we're telling the same story again and again, this is the story we're going to be telling – that in 2010 we won Album of the Year.'

She was so overloaded with Grammys that when she was posing for photographers with an armful of gold awards, she even managed to drop one and it broke. The event's organisers replaced it for her with a blank award.

Taylor was overwhelmed and elated, and it should have been the perfect start to the year, but instead of positive headlines the following morning when she picked up the papers, she was in the media for all the wrong reasons. It was an altogether different kind of hangover.

During the ceremony, she had taken to the stage to sing a medley of 'Today Was a Fairytale' and 'You Belong With

Me', and then duetted with rock singer Stevie Nicks, who joined her on stage for a lively rendition of the Fleetwood Mac song 'Rhiannon'. Many of the journalists in the audience noted that, in parts of her performances, she was out of tune. The venomous backlash started.

Entertainment Weekly claimed: 'The last thing I want to do is ruin another awards ceremony for Taylor Swift but there's no doubt that someone was badly off-key.' And the *Los Angeles Times* wrote: 'Swift gave a strikingly bad vocal performance . . . sounding tinny and rhythmically flat-footed as she shared the microphone with the distinctive Stevie Nicks . . . What Beyoncé may as well have been saying to Taylor Swift – "So you think you're a crossover artist? You ain't seen nothing kid."'

The *Washington Post* agreed: 'A night in the charmed life of Taylor Swift: Give an incredibly wretched vocal performance, go on to win the biggest Grammy of 2010 anyway.'

Taylor has never purported to be the perfect singer and just weeks before the event she revealed to the *Los Angeles Times* that she wasn't always insistent on sounding polished.

'It's really more about portraying the song in a way that gets the feeling across, rather than every phrase being exactly perfect,' she said. 'I think it's the writer in me that's a little more obsessed with the meaning of the song than the vocal technique. All that stuff is like math to me. Overthinking vocals and stuff – I never want to get to that point.'

Bloggers vented their thoughts and the public also took to Twitter to condemn her singing. Everyone was trying to push the golden girl off her gilded pedestal.

Scott Borchetta initially blamed an ear-volume problem and then was forced to defend the songstress again, telling the*Tennessean*: 'Maybe she's not the best technical singer, but she's probably the best emotional singer because everybody else who gets up there and is technically perfect, people don't seem to want more of it.'

He added to AP 'This is not *American Idol*. This is not a competition of getting up and seeing who can sing the highest note. This is about a true artist and writer and communicator. It's not about that technically perfect performance.' He argued that her unwillingness to rely on autotune, like so many other artists performing live, showed courage.

However, Scott's reference to the hit TV show just caused further anger and former *American Idol* winner Kelly Clarkson wrote on her blog: 'I understand defending your artist obviously because I have done the same in the past for artists I like, including Taylor, so you might see why it's upsetting to read you attacking *American Idol* for producing simply vocalists that hit "the high notes". Thank you for that "Captain Obvious" sense of humour because you know what, we not only hit the high notes, you forgot to mention we generally hit the "right" notes as well. Every artist has a bad performance or two and that is understandable, but throwing blame will not make the situation at hand any better.

'I have been criticized left and right for having shaky per-formances before (and they were shaky) and what my manager or label executives say to me and the public is "I'll kick butt next time" or "every performance isn't going to be perfect" . . . I bring this up because you should take a lesson from these people and instead of lashing out at other artists (that in your "humble" opinion lack true artistry), you should simply take a breath and realise that sometimes things won't go according to plan or work out and that's okay.'

It was just the start of the repercussions. Many commentators started to discuss Taylor's privileged upbringing and speculated that her parents had 'bought' her a record deal. There were even rumours that Taylor's father's money helped to set up Big Machine and he bought a mass quantity of her first album, and that explained why she was the label's biggest artist.

Then influential industry analyst Bob Lefsetz said that her career would dry up 'overnight' and advised Taylor and her people to hire a crisis management team as she was too 'young and dumb' to understand.

He penned: 'In one fell swoop, Taylor Swift consigned herself to the dustbin of teen phenoms. Who we expect to burn brightly and then fade away. From New Kids on the Block to Backstreet Boys to Miley Cyrus. A wall is created, stating you can't come any further. Debbie Gibson can appear in shows on Broadway, but she can't have a hit record, the powers-that-be won't let it happen.

'Taylor's too young and dumb to understand the mistake she made. And those surrounding her are addicted to cash and are afraid to tell her no. But last night, Taylor Swift SHOULD have auto-tuned. To save her career. They say it's easy to fake it in the twenty-first century. But one thing we know is the truth will always come out. It's hard to be a singer if you can't sing.'

One blogger on CMT ranted: 'Money can buy anything including a record contract. She can't sing and she's getting by on daddy's money, her looks and the cluelessness of the public ... they are so memorised by her youth and looks that they ignore her very poor singing ability.'

Another penned: 'Guess you haven't heard of what Scott Swift (Taylor Swift's father) spent to get her foot in the door huh? The stories are out there and Bob Lefsetz among others confirmed them. Swift's initial breakthrough may have come through social networking but the awards and the hype are definitely done by machine and let's not forget that her sophomore album has been marketed and distributed by the major label Universal Republic in partnership with Big Machine. As for the live performances, see Taylor Swift isn't doing mostly acoustic numbers in concert. She's doing full on big production pop rock numbers that she can't sing live without backup singers to cover for her and, if industry whispers are to be believed, live auto-tune or backing tracks.'

Taylor never denied her family's help in her success and while they gave her freedom to pursue her dreams, they certainly couldn't have given her any sort of head start in such a brutal industry. Fans came to her side and argued on websites and blogs that she had natural talent.

Her local paper, the *Tennessean*, argued: 'Remember the puzzles "What's wrong with this picture?" You search for all the faults ignoring the overall larger picture. Reference Taylor Swift. Multi-talented, she not only sings well enough to strike a chord with a huge audience, Taylor single-handedly introduced country music to a much-welcomed younger demographic and generated audience interest. She writes, dances, acts and is a dazzling performer . . .'

Scott Borchetta rallied to his top artist's side again, saying: 'I can tell you with absolute clarity that she is one of the most talented artists I have worked with in some twenty-five years in the business. Also, when starting the new label Big Machine and watching every dollar, I can factually tell you we made her record for a third of what major labels spend. There are tons of artists that come to town every year with tons of money, whether it's from investors or parents. You can't buy talent. You can't buy charisma. You can't buy songwriting skills. You can't buy a record deal at Big Machine . . . If you're jealous of Taylor's success and you're looking to tear her down, keep making this crap up . . . she's likely to be a star for a long time to come, so you might be smart to pick a fight you can win and a target you can successfully tear down – this ain't it!'

It must have been an agonising time for Taylor, who was fast realising the price of fame. She kept quiet, and stopped reading articles about herself because she found it too hard, even if they were not negative.

'Even if it's not bad, I think actively caring about people's daily perception of you makes you second-guess everything,' she told *Glamour*.

She tried to weather the storm and continued on the

Australian dates of her Fearless tour. She was also guest of honour at a private dinner with Scott Borchetta and representatives from the National Academy of Recording Arts and Sciences (who organise the Grammys) as well as people from the American Music Awards, the Country Music Association and the Academy of Country Music. The event was to celebrate *Fearless* being officially recognised as the most awarded album in the history of country music. It had gone triple platinum, with 13 million record sales and more than 25 million downloads.

Scott summed up the success story with a gushing speech, praising his protégée and trying to buoy her spirits.

'The eighteen months of our lives known as the Fearless era have been history-making, euphoric and triumphant. The sales, the airplay, the accolades and the awards have been incredible. But, most important to me is that my friend Taylor and her collective team of family, record label, management, and her road family continue to raise the bar with work ethic, achievement and enjoyment. Dreams do come true.'

However, the impact of what had been said about her Grammys performance was lasting and Taylor was deeply hurt. She kept her feelings to herself and only shared them with her closest allies, who she stuck close to.

'It's weird – I thought I'd have so many more friends, but I feel like I'm less popular than I've ever been,' she said to *Teen Vogue*. 'It makes me value the people I can trust even more; I still have the same best friend I had all through high school.'

She often went to visit Abigail, who was studying journalism at Kansas City, and her brother Austin, who was at business school, to take stock and focus on how far she had come.

Talking to MTV's *The Seven*, she said: 'I go and visit my brother at college and visit my best friend Abigail at college and I attend her journalism class. I have no regrets about that path that I took, but I still try to experience as much as I can out of life. Loving this is a big part of my life and sometimes, if you get too tired or you're jetlagged you might forget. But I always remind myself that I love this.'

Her family supported her one hundred per cent and Taylor revealed that even though they spent a lot of time apart, she often went to her brother for advice, telling a radio station: 'I have my girlfriends and we talk about everything. But one person who I go to for advice, who is a guy, is my brother. He gives me really straightforward advice. Nine times out of ten, when I say, "What should I do?" he says, "Well, what do you want to do?" That answer is always really easy; what you want to do is what you should do. He's younger, it's so weird, he's so wise!'

If anyone needed more proof of Taylor's appeal, *Valentine's Day* was released and coined over $50 million at the box office. Even though she was only on screen for about ten minutes many reviewers sought her out.

CMT.com wrote: 'Swift makes the most of limited time and is – quite unsurprisingly – a dynamic screen presence whom the camera clearly adores. You might think of her extended cameo as a high-profile, low-pressure screen test for bigger and better roles, and she passes with flying colours.' She later picked up a Teen Choice Award for Movie Breakout Female.

Other critics were less kind about the film, with *Rolling Stone* labelling it 'the date movie from hell'; but Taylor wasn't bothered because she wasn't planning to embark on a career in Hollywood.

'Being involved in a movie was cool,' she explained, 'but I prefer the pay-off of a crowd screaming. So much of my happiness comes from the reaction of the audience, which is why I'm looking forward to my next record and tour.'

In February, rumours started to gather pace that Taylor was dating fellow singer John Mayer. Rock and pop singer-song-writer John was twelve years her senior and a notorious womaniser, who had had a number of high-profile romances with the likes of Jennifer Aniston, Jessica Simpson and Cameron Diaz. He was well known for his rock-'n'-roll lifestyle and open approach to women.

Talking about Jessica Simpson, whom he dated on and off for ten months, `from August 2006, he told *Playboy* she was like 'a drug'.

'That girl, for me, is a drug,' he said. 'And drugs aren't good for you if you do lots of them. Yeah, that girl is like crack cocaine to me. Sexually it was crazy. That's all I'll say. It was like napalm. Sexual napalm. Did you ever say "I want to quit my life and just f***ing snort you?"'

He was outspoken about his love of porn, declaring: 'When I watch porn, if it's not hot enough, I'll make up back stories in my mind. My biggest dream is to write pornography.' When he was asked about dating black women, he responded: 'My dick is sort of like a white supremacist. I've got a Benetton heart and a fuckin' David Duke cock. I'm going to start dating separately from my dick.'

He also spoke candidly about Jennifer Aniston, who he split with in March 2009 after a ten-month fling, admitting during an impromptu press conference outside a New York gym that it was him who dumped her.

He said to a crowd of journalists: 'Have me as a man who ended a relationship stand here and write some truth. Have me stand up for somebody and write that Jennifer Aniston is the smartest, most sophisticated person I think I've ever met. She's one of the most lovely people I've ever met in my life and I'm going through something that's a very personal thing and you have to give that up . . . There's no lying, there's no cheating. There's no nothing . . . I don't waste people's time.'

The actress, who had doggedly tried to avoid the paparazzi since her failed marriage to Brad Pitt, was furious with him. However, he later wormed his way back into the *Friends'* star's life, with Jen telling *Vogue* that he would never publicly talk about their romance again. A year later they called it quits again after he reportedly became obsessed with Twitter. He later tweeted: 'This heart didn't come with instructions.'

To say John was everything Taylor wasn't would be an understatement, but she was definitely in awe of her fellow singer and it's no wonder it set the gossip magazines into overdrive. A year before the alleged romance, Taylor had spoken about her admiration for the singer to *People* magazine after they met at an event:

'I was starstruck by the fact that he came up and introduced himself to me,' she laughed. 'I just respect him so much, I was rattling off quotes that he said in his blog, and he was probably like thinking that I'm a stalker. But he was amazing and sweet.'

John returned the compliment and told her he had been watching her progress.

'I was like, "What, you know my name?"' she continued. 'I'm such a fan of his writing and everything so it was really cool to get to meet one of my heroes.'

The couple began collaborating together on 'Half of My Heart', a song on Mayer's 2009 album *Battle Studies* and she was seen sitting on his lap in the recording studio.

'Her arms were around him, and she was talking in his ear,' a source told hollywoodlife.com. 'They were acting like teenagers.'

That night, they reportedly ate dinner out with friends before spending the night together at John's suite in the Hermitage Hotel in Nashville.

The mole continued: 'Taylor spent the night and enjoyed mid-morning room service before leaving his suite the next day.'

Reps for both parties denied the meeting had taken place at all. However, it soon became clear something was definitely going on and when he was asked how the hook-up went, John hardly denied it, replying: 'How do you think it went?'

The *National Enquirer* said Taylor's mum, Andrea, was seriously unhappy with her daughter's latest choice, pulling the singer to one side and telling him to stay away from Taylor.

'Andrea has told John point-blank to back off,' a source said. 'All John could do was to offer Andrea a compliment on raising a lovely daughter. He said he understood completely, and it was an honour enough to call Taylor his friend. She said a friendship was fine, but there was no way he'd get close enough to Taylor to break her heart if she had anything to say about it.'

Despite Andrea's pep talk, when they did break up soon after, Taylor was clearly upset and in true Taylor form, she penned a song, 'Dear John', which featured on her next album. The CD booklet contained the message of the song, which read: I LOVED YOU FROM THE VERY FIRST DAY.

While Taylor never confirmed that the song was about John, she only explained: 'A lot of times when people's relationships end, they write an email to that person and say everything that they wish they would have said. A lot of times they don't push send . . . This one was a tough one to write, and I guess putting it on the album was pushing send.'

Later, John told *Rolling Stone* that he hadn't known about the song, which made him feel 'terrible'.

'As a songwriter . . . I think it's kind of cheap songwriting,' he argued. 'I know she's the biggest thing in the world, and I'm not trying to sink anybody's ship, but I think it's abusing your talent to rub your hands together and go, "Wait till he gets a load of this!" That's bullshit. I didn't deserve it. I'm pretty good at taking accountability now, and I never did anything to deserve that. It was a really lousy thing for her to do . . . I never got an email. I never got a phone call. I was really caught off-guard, and it really humiliated me at a time when I'd already been dressed down. I mean, how would you feel if, at the lowest you've ever been, someone kicked you even lower?'

On 1 May 2010, it started to rain in Nashville. Heavy at first, the rain soon turned torrential and continued for several days. The damage was huge, with thirty people killed and thousands left homeless. The place Taylor regarded as her home ended up barely resembling the one she knew. Many of her fellow musicians lost their beloved guitars and musical equipment.

'Being at home during the storm, I honestly could not believe what was happening to the city and the people I love so dearly,' Taylor told AP. 'Nashville is my home, and the reason why I get to do what I love. I have always been proud to be a Nashvillian, but especially now, seeing the love that runs through this city when there are people in crisis.'

The singer tweeted about the destruction the flooding had brought to one of Nashville's landmarks: 'Please keep Nashville in your heart. Seeing a picture of the Grand Ole Opry halfway underwater was a kind of heartbreak I can't describe.'

The locals organised a telethon, and Taylor generously donated a huge $500,000 to the clean-up effort.

She said: 'It was the craziest thing that I've ever seen. I was at my house in Hendersonville; we were staring out the window, thinking it didn't seem like rain. It just seemed like something in a movie. It was really emotional for me because those are the streets I learned to drive on. People's houses are just ruined. It was so heartbreaking to see that in my town, the place that I call home, and the place that I feel most safe. I just send my love to my friends and neighbours who got hit harder than I did.'

Throughout her career, Taylor has donated to victims of natural disasters, including pledging $100,000 to victims of the Iowa flood in 2008, featuring in a Hope for Haiti telethon and recording a song for an album helping the island.

The same week as the Nashville floods, Taylor was in New York for the annual glitzy Met Gala, where she shone in an angelic Ralph Lauren gown. She was then at No. 9 on *Time* magazine's 'Most Influential' list, alongside Simon Cowell, Robert Pattinson and Ricky Gervais, and was determined to spread the word that the people of Nashville needed help.

Taking to the microphone during her performance, she said: 'Before we play our last song, I would just love it if I could give a shout-out in the room where we have the most influential people in the world. Nashville just had the worst storm that we've ever seen in the history of the city and the Grand Ole Opry is under water. So if you could please keep Nashville in your thoughts or prayers that would be wonderful. I really appreciate it.'

Critics and bloggers could say what they liked about Taylor, but she was determined to stick by her mantra: 'No matter what happens in life, be good to people. Because being nice is a wonderful legacy to leave behind.'

CHAPTER EIGHT

'These songs are made up of words I didn't say when the moment was right in front of me'

With the celebrity spotlight firmly shining down on her every move, Taylor had been busy writing while living the ups and downs of fame and, in July, *Billboard* announced that her next album would be called *Speak Now* and would be released in October, with the lead single dropping at the end of August. Unlike her previous two albums, Taylor had written every one of the fourteen tracks herself and described the new release as 'a collection of confessions – things I wish I had said when I was in the moment'.

During a live webcast, she explained: 'I actually wrote all the songs myself [but] it didn't really happen on purpose, it just sort of happened. Like, I'd get my best ideas at 3 a.m. in Arkansas and I didn't have a co-writer around.'

As Scott Borchetta pointed out, it would be a pretty amazing feat if she could pull a brilliant third album out the bag.

'Look, if she can produce a superior third album, one that's as big as the last two ... well, when's the last time somebody did that?'

While everything else in her life was meticulously planned down to the hour and minute, such was her busy schedule, the release of her lead single was anything but straightforward. She was relaxing on a plane to Japan when someone from her record label approached her and broke the news.

She told *Entertainment Weekly*: 'The release of my first single was nothing like I expected it to be, because I like things to be structured and planned and orderly. And I've never known any kind of release other than, you plan the date it's going to come out and that's the day that you release it and that's what happens. When I got on that plane, I just thought I was going to Japan, and I thought it was going to be a regular flight – watch a few movies, take a nap. But an hour into the flight, one of my managers came up to me and said, "Hey, so, try not to panic. But how would you feel about a release of the single on August 5? So that's 8/5. And eight plus five is 13, which is your lucky number!" I said, "It leaked, didn't it?" And she said, "Yes."'

A low-quality MP3 version of the song 'Mine' had been recorded and put online. In order to make sure it was the polished version that people were listening to, her record company had no choice but to release it early. Taylor knew there was nothing she could do to control it so she rolled with the new schedule. She had learned her lesson that all publicity could be spun into positive press.

'Mine' was a catchy, coming-of-age song about a boy from her past, similar to her up-tempo hits 'Love Story' and 'You Belong to Me'.

'It's a song that's about my tendency to run from love,' she explained. 'Every really direct example of love I've had in front of me has ended in goodbye and in break-ups and things like that, so I've developed this pattern of running away when it comes time to fall in love and stay in a relationship and this song is about finding an exception to that and finding the person that makes you believe in love and realise that it can work out.'

Fortunately, the video, which had been shot on a private estate in Portland, was ready to go.

She landed to a barrage of congratulations texts and phone calls, and tweeted: 'I landed in Japan and got 20 texts and looked at iTunes and got tears in my eyes. And so, we begin again :)'

The impact of 'Mine' on the *Billboard* Country chart was immediate and it debuted in the third place in its first week, selling an astonishing 1,047,000 copies. No one had sold that many singles since 50 Cent's 'The Massacre' back in 2005.

Taylor was busier than ever, gearing up for another whirlwind tour of performances and promotions.

'I'm obsessed with being busy. It's hectic and non-stop,' she said. 'But I'm so ready.'

However, she also tried to protect the small things in her life that made her happy and feel normal. She insisted once again that fame wouldn't change her and she was open to criticism.

'As your career grows, the list of things that makes you happy should not become smaller, it should become bigger,' she told *USA Today*. 'You can't cross off walking in the park. You can't cross off talking to people, just because you're talking to more people. I still love all the things I used to love, I just love more things. There is a tendency to want to get thick-skinned. There is a tendency to block out negative things, because they really hurt. But if I stop feeling pain, then I'm afraid I'll stop feeling immense excitement and epic celebration and happiness. I can't stop feeling those things, so I feel everything. And that keeps me who I am.'

The anticipation surrounding *Speak Now* was huge but Taylor did her best to distance herself from the high expectations.

'I have a lot of anxiety about things on certain days, but I have anxiety because I care,' she said to Reuters. 'It's not anxiety that's crippling. It's a five-minute conversation with myself about if a [sales] number really defines this piece of art that I've created and what that means, and what the number's going to be. I try to predict what it's going to be, and then I realise that I can't predict what it's going to be, and then I sit there and say something to myself like, "Well, you're happy today. Enjoy this and be proud of the music that you've made."'

The new album marked a change in direction for the young star and she was at a key point in her career. She no longer daydreamed about boys and being rescued by her real-life Romeo. The record addressed more mature subjects, like navigating complex relationships and moving out of home.

'At one point, the record was not called *Speak Now*. It was called *Enchanted*,' Scott Borchetta said. 'We were at lunch, and she had played me a bunch of the new songs. I looked at her and I'm like, "Taylor, this record isn't about fairy-tales and high school any more. That's not where you're at. I don't think the record should be called *Enchanted*."'

Taylor left the table and, by the time she came back, she had dreamed up the name *Speak Now*.

'I'm just fascinated by people – how they live their lives, what they live their lives for,' she said. 'It's just a never-ending thought process for me about how we end up where we are – and where we're going.'

It also marked a change in musical direction and was a clear departure from the country style that had informed her earlier work – it was far more of a pop rock album.

It shipped more than 2 million copies in its first week of release – no album had sold more than a million copies since Lil' Wayne's *Tha Carter III* in June 2008. At the end of the first week of release, Taylor tweeted: 'I . . . Can't . . . Believe . . . This . . . You guys have absolutely lit up my world. Thank you.'

It was hailed as a triumph by the critics.

Rolling Stone said: 'Swift's third album, *Speak Now*, is roughly twice as good as her 2006 debut. These 14 tunes chronicle the hopes and dreams of boy-crazy small-town Everygirls, and Swift wrote them all by herself. (She also

co-produced *Speak Now* with Nathan Chapman, who over-
saw Swift's first two albums.)

'Swift might be a clever Nashville pro who knows all the
hit-making tricks, but she's also a high-strung, hyper-roman-
tic gal with a melodramatic streak the size of the Atchafalaya
Swamp. So she's in a class by herself when it comes to turning all that romantic turmoil into great songs. At this point,
she's like the new Morrissey except with even more eyeliner.'

USA Today added: 'What do you do when your star soars
so high that fans expect the moon, while critics call you over-
rated and overexposed? If you're smart, and Taylor Swift is
certainly that, you remind everyone what all the fuss was
about in the first place. In Swift's case, that's her songwriting. The 20-year-old phenom crafted the 14 tracks on *Speak
Now* by herself, and like the tunes on 2008's *Fearless*, they're
at once precocious and candidly, refreshingly youthful in
their perspective.'

And Europe started to get excited, too. The *Guardian* called
it a 'triumph', adding: '*Speak Now* is a conscious attempt to
move beyond those childish things while retaining her balance
of maturity and relatability. At times the self-consciousness of
an artist forcing herself into new modes shows – but mostly,
Speak Now is a triumph. 'Mine' reprises the joyous rush of
Swift's breakthrough hit, 'Love Story', but depicts love as an
adult process rather than a teenage dream. The hazy crush of
'Enchanted' showcases Swift's instinct for capturing emotion
with astonishing exactitude – right down to the dread sneak-
ing in at the song's close.'

However, it was *Speak Now*'s confessions surrounding her

personal life that got the media whipped into a frenzy. Journalists and bloggers started to pick apart the songs looking for clues on who the tracks were about, including 'Dear John', a biting open letter to her ex, John Mayer, and 'Back to December', a wistful apology to Taylor Lautner. As usual, in her CD booklet, Taylor capitalised seemingly random letters in the printed lyrics for each song, and as usual, the capitalisations were not random at all. They spelled out sometimes cryptic, sometimes obvious 'secret' messages, usually about who or what inspired the tune. She said she felt that the coded messages brought her closer to her fans.

Speaking to National Public Radio, she said: 'The first thing that I think about when I'm writing my lyrics is directly communicating with the person the song is about. I think what I've learned recently is that it's not ... heartbreak that inspires my songs. It's not love that inspires my songs. It's individual people that come into my life. I've had relationships with people that were really substantial and meant a lot to me, but I couldn't write a song about that person for some reason. Then again, you'll meet someone that comes into your life for two weeks and you write an entire record about them.

'When I first started writing songs, I was always scared that my songs were too personal – like, if I put someone's name in a song, people won't relate to it as much. But what I saw happening was, if I let my fans into my life and my feelings and what I'm going through – my vulnerabilities, my fears, my insecurities – it turns out they have all those things, too, and it kind of connects us.'

In the prologue to *Speak Now*, she explained the overall theme of the album.

'I think most of us fear reaching the end of our life, and looking back regretting the moments we didn't speak up. When we didn't say, "I love you." When we should've said, "I'm sorry." When we didn't stand up for ourselves or someone who needed help. These songs are made up of words I didn't say when the moment was right in front of me.

'These songs are open letters. Each is written with a specific person in mind, telling them what I meant to tell them in person. To the beautiful boy whose heart I broke in December. To my first love who I never thought would be my first heartbreak. To my band. To a mean man I used to be afraid of. To someone who made my world very dark for a while. To a girl who stole something of mine. To someone I forgive for what he said in front of the whole world.

'Words can break someone into a million pieces, but they can also put them back together. I hope you use yours for good, because the only words you'll regret more than the ones left unsaid are the ones you use to intentionally hurt someone.'

She signed off, 'Love Taylor' and 'ps to all the boys who inspired this album, you should've known. ;)'

One of the bigger revelations came in the secret message alongside 'The Story of Us', a song about awkwardly bumping into someone and avoiding an awards show. Many people presumed that Taylor Lautner was the focus after they had an awkward moment facing each other at the

People's Choice Awards, just weeks after breaking up. However, in the booklet, the letters spelled C-M-T-A-W-A-R-D-S, suggesting it was about John Mayer, who was at the CMT Awards.

Another person came in for criticism in 'Mean'.

'"Mean" is about a writer who kept going off at me, blasting me,' she said. 'There's a place for constructive criticism, but then there's a line that gets crossed. Every time I read something new, it would just level me, and my only way of handling it was to write a song about it.'

Many critics suggested that the song was about industry insider Bob Lefsetz, who had publicly humiliated her with his poisonous words about her appearance at the Grammys.

The track 'Enchanted' also attracted some speculation, with references to an unnamed guy and her code spelling out the name Adam. Soon, journalists had homed in on Owl City's Adam Young.

He told *Us Weekly*: 'I bought the record when it came out and I was playing it top to bottom. I love the classic adding up the letters in lyrics. I got to the song ["Enchanted"] and I had to take a step back and decipher the code. I was like, "This song is about me!"'

When the pair eventually met, sadly it wasn't the fairy tale they had both been hoping for.

'I'm not the most romantic and eloquent guy in the world,' he said. 'She's just this endearing, wonderful girl and maybe I said something wrong . . . She's a superstar and I'm just a kid from a small town in the middle of nowhere, so I felt like a peasant in the presence of a princess.'

He was clearly taken by the star and, on the following Valentine's Day, he wrote her a message on his website, saying: 'Everything about you is lovely. You're an immensely charming girl with a beautiful heart and more grace and elegance than I know how to describe.'

Another song that everyone talked about was 'Innocent'. Taylor wasn't going to let the Kanye incident pass her by and the track indicated that she had forgiven him, but also pointed towards his immaturity, with the words: 'It's okay, life is a tough crowd/32, and still growin' up now/Who you are is not what you did/You're still innocent.'

Taylor told MTV: 'I think a lot of people expected me to write a song about [Kanye]. But, for me, it was important to write a song to him. It doesn't really add anything good if I start victimizing myself and complaining about things. Because I'm proud of that performance at the VMAs last year, where my fans helped me get through it. And there was a lot that went down backstage that I will always be thankful for, and the fans in the subway know exactly what happened that night. I feel everything. I've never had this thick skin that can't be ... It's not like I am bulletproof in any sense of the word.'

Taylor was showing off her less angelic side: 'Better than Revenge' was said to be about actress Camilla Belle, who dated her ex, Joe Jonas. The lyrics suggested she was known for her prowess in bed, rather than her acting skills, perhaps in retaliation to the stories that Joe had split with Taylor because she was 'frigid'.

While she never confirmed the song was about the pretty

actress, she alluded to the fact it was her on Twitter. When gossip columnist Perez tweeted her with: '@taylorswift13 The song about Camilla Belle is ... wow. Love it!' Taylor replied, '@PerezHilton Thank you so much for the love!! Feel like dancing around.' If Camilla was in any doubt about the subject, that exchange seemed to speak for itself.

But she loved keeping everyone guessing and told the *Daily Telegraph*: 'I'm the only person who knows who [my songs] are really about and there's a comfort in that.'

Taylor had made a surprise appearance at the MTV Video Music Awards in LA in September, the month prior to the release of *Speak Now*. It was a year since KanyeGate and to make a point, she chose to sing her track 'Innocent' in a simple white dress. Moments from the confrontation were screened before the camera panned to a darkly lit Taylor, who started strumming on her steel guitar. Kanye also sang a new track, 'Runaway', and much of the media took the opportunity to weigh in on whether the evening's performances had settled the score between them.

Speaking about the R&B star, the *New York Times* said: 'Wearing a red suit, he looked amateurish and vulnerable, and also affecting. At the end, Mr. West's knowing, bombastic humility won ... Ms. Swift – victim, but no naïf – performed a new song, 'Innocent', directed at Mr. West, an extremely savvy insult masquerading as the high road. She performed it with minimal accompaniment, barefoot, and with an unsteady relationship to pitch.'

Entertainment Weekly added: 'She seems to have forgiven

him. She looked gorgeous, as she is wont to do, but, um, the actual song was a pretty opaque,' while *Time* summed up: 'In reality, they're both winners – even if one of their performances was a disaster, they could console themselves by taking a swim in their pool full of money.'

As the albums flooded out of mass-market outlets, Taylor also sold a deluxe version of the CD through Walmart, in which she starred in her own funny and touching TV ad. In it, she wore goofy false teeth and had huge frizzy hair, parodying her teenage self, in a Dolly Parton-style purple trouser suit and wig.

To mark the release she performed a collection of songs in the middle of New York's Central Park. She even had a grand piano brought outside and was backed by a full orchestra. The performance was screened live across MTV, the Country Music Channel and VH1. She also sang on the *Today* show and David Letterman's *Late Show*.

October also saw her first-ever *People* magazine cover, in which she dished on all the men who inspired her music, saying: 'I will say everything in my music. Sometimes when things impact you so intensely, it takes writing a song to get over them.'

John Mayer had broken Taylor's heart and now she had exacted her revenge: she was free to move on.

On the same day her album hit the stores, the Internet was buzzing with rumours of a new romance after Taylor was seen backstage with *Brokeback Mountain* star Jake Gyllenhaal at a recording of *Saturday Night Live* in Manhattan, where she was supporting her actress friend, Emma Stone. Taylor had met Emma in 2008 at an event for *Hollywood Life* magazine and they had grown close, uniquely understanding each other and the pressures of fame.

A source told *People*: 'They [Taylor and Jake] showed up together. They walked around together backstage but they were careful not to be seen too close. It was hard to tell if they were together, but everyone was shocked that she brought him.'

Tongues started wagging again when they were seen walking around Brooklyn together, before stopping at a restaurant for brunch. Jake, who was twenty-nine at the time, had split with his last girlfriend, actress Reese Witherspoon, ten months previously, after two years together.

Everyone wanted to know if this romance was official and, while Taylor was on *The Ellen DeGeneres Show* promoting *Speak Now*, the comedienne asked her if she felt optimistic about love.

Taylor replied: 'Well, why wouldn't anyone be?' and Ellen cheekily shot back: 'Especially if your boyfriend is Jake Gyllenhaal, because he's very handsome. Y'all are just hanging out though right?' Taylor didn't deny – or confirm the romance, and said: 'You have a picture of us on the screen, don't you?'

She was also coy about 'Dear John', saying the song 'could be' about John as that is 'kind of what it is'.

'Okay, great,' Ellen replied. 'We know the answer now. It's about him [John Mayer]. You didn't dispute it so obviously.' Ellen had succeeded where many other journalists had failed in trying to get the young star to talk about her relationships.

In November, Hollywood star Gwyneth Paltrow confirmed that she had acted as matchmaker and hosted a dinner for the hot new couple in London. The actress had starred with the actor in *Proof* in 2005 and told *USA Today*: 'I've known Jake for a long time and he's a great guy, and Chris [Martin, Gwyneth's husband] has a friendship with Taylor.'

Jake and Taylor went on to spend their Thanksgiving holiday in New York together after the singer cancelled her plans to spend the time at home with her own family.

'Jake invited her to New York for Thanksgiving,' an insider told *Us Weekly*. 'It wasn't planned in advance but she said, "Why not? I can do it, and I'm going." Her parents weren't thrilled. But she explained to them that she gets to see them all the time and wasn't able to spend much time with Jake during the publicity madness. She loves his family and he loves hers.'

During the holiday, she met Jake's family, including his sister Maggie Gyllenhaal and her husband Peter Sarsgaard and their daughter Ramona, and she was happy to pull her weight around their home.

'There was no diva behaviour,' the source continued. 'She pitched in to cook and clear the dishes. She seemed very interested in his family and asked them lots of questions about themselves.'

Taylor and Jake were then seen sipping maple-syrup lattes in Brooklyn, before they hopped on a plane to Taylor's hometown in Nashville, where they were spotted cosying up at another coffee shop and giggling over ice cream.

'They were smiling and laughing,' a fellow diner told *People*. 'They were talking a lot and enjoying each other's company. They didn't look like just friends. They were not trying to be discreet by any means. They were definitely a couple.'

Jake was busy promoting his latest film *Love & Other Drugs* and there were reports he had spent £100,000 having Taylor flown out to London's exclusive Dorchester hotel on a private jet so they could spent two days holed up together with room service.

The pair were next pictured together at the start of December and sources said that the romance was going from strength to strength.

'Taylor is smitten. She loves how nice and affectionate he is,' an insider told *Us Weekly*. 'Jake likes that Taylor is sweet, low-key and very easy to be around.'

Taylor was also busy with the normal round of award ceremonies. Attending the American Music Awards, she turned heads with a new blunter, poker straight haircut and a short, rocky rhinestone dress. Katy Perry tweeted her afterwards, saying: 'Gurl your hair looked amazeballs.'

Taylor won the Favorite Country Female Artist and performed 'Back to December', playing a piano sitting in the open under a night sky, amidst trees decorated with Christmas lights, dressed in super-skinny black trousers and a sharp blazer. This seemed like a deliberate move towards a rockier image and away from her natural country roots.

By now, she was a seasoned awards winner but she still admitted she got nervous when performing, telling *Teen Vogue*: 'I do, but only if I'm not sure what the audience thinks of me, like at awards shows. I never look down at the front row! My heroes watching equals nerves!'

As Taylor's twenty-first birthday approached, reports emerged saying Jake had come up trumps and bought her an $11,000 vintage Gretsch guitar, signed by country-music star Chet Atkins, a legendary American guitarist and record producer who helped create what is known as the 'Nashville sound', a smooth form of country music. Jake was a proper gentleman and had first thought about it when Taylor said how much she loved the brand when they were in Nashville one day.

If the guitar wasn't generous enough, *In Touch* magazine said he splashed out on an 'Oscar-worthy' white-gold bracelet costing $100,000, set with nearly 30 carats of colourless diamonds. He also bought her some Kona coffee, a coffee grinder and a coffeemaker – and even made her a card.

While twenty-one is a monumental date for most young Americans because it marks the legal drinking age, Taylor wasn't suddenly going to change her clean-living ways.

'I don't think I'm going to all of the sudden start being in love with the idea of going to a club,' she told *People*. 'I like to dance around and have fun with my friends and we have a blast, but I've never really felt compelled to be drunk and I don't think that's terribly awful.'

She added: 'It'll be cool that I'll be able to go to a lot of concerts that my friends always go to and I sit at home because it's twenty-one and over.'

On her birthday, Taylor spent the day at a Nashville radio station and then prepared food for 70-odd guests who attended her Christmas-themed birthday party. They nibbled on sushi and home-prepared canapés, before Taylor handed out thank-you gifts to her friends and members of her management team. However, Jake was noticeable in his absence and was apparently back in LA. Over Christmas, Taylor jetted to the Turks and Caicos for a much-needed two-day break with her mum and brother.

There were no more sightings of Jake and Taylor and soon reports indicated the actor, who was intensely private, had ended things over the phone because the pressure of having another high-profile relationship had become too much.

Us Weekly claimed: 'He said he wasn't feeling it anymore and was uncomfortable with all the attention they got. He also said he could feel the age difference. Taylor is really upset. We told her not to move so fast with this but she didn't listen.'

Some sceptics argued that the relationship was a publicity stunt, while some magazines said she was heartbroken, saying she had stopped eating and spent all her time in the gym frantically working out to try and ease her heartache.

Whatever the reason for the split it had obviously hit Taylor hard and it was more than a year later when she admitted how heartbroken she had been.

She told *Vogue* the following year: 'I got nothing going on!

I just don't really feel like dating. I really have this great life right now, and I'm not sad and I'm not crying this Christmas, so I am really stoked about that. I am not gonna go into it! It's a sad story!'

She added that she couldn't understand his view about privacy, adding: 'Also, I can't deal with someone who's obsessed with privacy. People kind of care if there are two famous people dating. But no one cares that much. If you care about privacy to the point where we need to dig a tunnel under this restaurant so that we can leave? I can't do that.'

Whatever happened with Jake, the publicity sparked by the split certainly didn't affect her sales. At the close of 2010, *Speak Now* was firmly at the top of the charts and Taylor was named as the top-selling artist of the year by *Billboard*, after shifting 4.4 million albums. She was also their most-played artist for the second year running and dominated their digital downloads with 34 million downloads. Again, *Forbes* named her in their list of the highest-earning celebrities of the year, with estimated earnings that year of a mind-boggling $45 million.

As well as revenue from her music, she became the latest face of *CoverGirl*.

'I have admired many of the CoverGirls since I was a little girl . . . great artists and actresses who are confident and still themselves,' she said in a press release. 'It's like a dream come true to be a part of the future of *CoverGirl*.'

Talking about feeling beautiful, she told website Glam: 'Based on some of the choices they've made, like Drew Barrymore, Ellen [DeGeneres], and Rihanna, they're all these different kinds of beautiful, I just thought it would be really cool to be part of a family that thinks that individuality is beautiful . . . When I feel really confident; I think it's a spontaneous thing that happens every once in a while and I can never predict when, but there are sometimes when I just feel really confident, smiling and laughing . . . I think in those [moments] when you do feel confident you should just live it up and appreciate it for the fact that it's there, because I don't think anybody is ever consistently always confident.'

She added to the *New York Times* that she would never champion something she didn't believe in.

'I don't believe in endorsing a product that you don't want to endorse. I've always wanted to be a CoverGirl. I've always wanted to have a fragrance, and so when it comes time to go on *Good Morning America* and wake up really early in the morning to promote that fragrance I'm going to do it with a smile on my face.'

The year 2011 began with the People's Choice Awards, on 5 January, where Taylor glowed in a pretty dress by J. Mendel and Prada shoes. She got the chance to present an award to Johnny Depp for Favorite Movie Actor for his role in *Pirates of the Caribbean* and also picked up the People's Choice Award for Favorite Country Artist from Sir Elton John. She thanked her fans for 'always being people I can count on', which could be interpreted as a veiled dig at her recent ex.

If it was, Taylor wasn't angry for too long. After the show, she tweeted a joke photo of her in the car with long-time friend Selena Gomez.

She wrote: 'Thank you SO much for the People's Choice Award! It's sitting here all sparkly in my hotel room. I love you guys. :)'

Selena, who is a pop singer and actress, is two and a half years younger than Taylor. The pair met and hit it off at a Jonas Brothers gig in 2008. Since then, they have spent a lot of time together having fun, shopping, going for dinner and having girly nights in. Despite their busy touring schedules, they always make time to see each other.

'She's like my little sister, you know?' Taylor said in a radio interview. 'I have never had such a truly sister-like relationship with someone, and it's so cool and really amazing to have a friend for that long. We met when I was like seventeen, eighteen ... so it is amazing with so much going on in our lives that we have stayed so close.'

Talking about her BFF's attributes, Taylor explained to the Brazilian magazine *Capricho*: 'She's so trustworthy, never judges you and knows how to listen.'

Talking about what she loves about Taylor, Selena told Z103.5: 'She's got this humour about her that's really funny. Whenever I come to her and I'm upset about something, she always finds a way to turn it into a comedy. She's just great. She's definitely one who will talk you through any problems you have.'

Not only that, the girls have similar tastes in music – which has proven to be very helpful during break-ups:

'Whenever we went through kind of our break-up

phase, we made each other playlists, so we'd email all these different songs we'd like and it went on for like three months,' Selena explained, adding, 'But it really helped; it was fun!'

During another split, Selena told Ryan Seacrest: 'She came to my house at ten thirty at night and knocked on my door. I opened it, and she had two big bags of junk food, cookies, Snickers and soda. She put it on the table, put her laptop on, we made a video, and she told me that now we could look forward to break-ups, since we know the other one will get us junk food.'

Along with Emma Stone, Selena is one of Taylor's closest friends and the three are often seen out together.

Talking to Popsugar website, Taylor revealed: 'They can predict my thoughts; I've known them for so long it's really cool to have friends that are that close . . . We all have crazy schedules but we make our time together count, and laugh and have hilarious dinners. It's nice to have people I consider trustworthy, great friends.'

One thing was certain: all the experiences she was having were making Taylor grow up fast.

'I've apparently been the victim of growing up, which apparently happens to all of us at one point or another,' she wrote. 'It's been going on for quite some time now, without me knowing it. I've found that growing up can mean a lot of things. For me, it doesn't mean I should become somebody completely new and stop loving the things I used to love. It means I've just added more things to my list . . . I've loved my fans from the very first day, but they've said things and done things recently that make me feel like they're my friends – more now than ever before. I'll never go a day without thinking about our memories together.'

CHAPTER NINE

'I didn't want to tell one big story. I wanted each song to have its own story'

If her Fearless tour was a dramatic spectacle, her fans hadn't seen anything yet.

In February 2011, Taylor would embark on another gruelling run of dates to promote *Speak Now*, playing an astonishing 111 nights across 19 countries in America, Asia, Europe and Australasia. It was her first tour performing in huge stadiums, with some venues packing in over 50,000 people per night. It was going to be bigger and better than anything her fans had ever seen.

She said: 'I'm so excited to go back out on tour again in 2011! The Fearless tour was so much fun and even more unforgettable than I ever imagined, and I can't wait to get back out and play my new music from *Speak Now*! The fans have been so amazing and I'm thrilled to play in new cities around the world and meet even more of my fans in 2011.'

With such a huge task ahead, critics might have questioned whether the star would burn out, but Taylor was not concerned.

'As far as burning out, I get tired a lot, but I never get tired of it,' she explained to *Marie Claire* magazine. 'I remember when I was a little kid and I used to sit there and think about how lucky I would be one day where people cared about the words that I wrote or how lucky I would be if someday I was just walking through the mall and saw some little girl walking by with my face on her T-shirt. When you spend so much time daydreaming about things like that, when that actually happens you don't ever complain about it. When I go to a restaurant, yeah I know that a line is probably going to form in front of the table, but didn't I always wish for that? Yeah, I did. So it's like, I never want to be the girl who wanted something so bad her whole life and then gets it and complains about it. I'm not going to be that girl.'

Taylor didn't receive any nominations for the 53rd Grammy Awards as *Speak Now* was released a few weeks after the deadlines set for nominations, meaning that it couldn't be considered until the 2012 awards, and she didn't attend because she was in Japan at the time. No doubt, after the previous year, she was happy to avoid the drama of the huge show.

At the end of the month there were reports of a new boyfriend in her life: Chord Overstreet – Sam Evans in Glee. They were seen first at an LA Kings hockey game together and then at Harvey Weinstein's exclusive pre-Oscars party. It seemed Taylor was the perfect choice for Chord, who said to *V* magazine his ideal date was 'funny, sweet, likes to laugh and is a good girl,' adding, 'she needs to have a taste for country music. And she has to be from the South. She doesn't have to be but there's nothing like Southern food.'

However, later that year, Hot Chelle Rae singer Ryan Follese, whose bandmate is Chord's brother, said fame was to blame for the rumours and they never officially had a relationship and were 'just hanging out'.

Back in 2010, Taylor had even been briefly linked to Chord's *Glee* castmate, the late Cory Monteith, who played William McKinley High School resident jock, Finn Hudson. After they were seen together at a bowing alley, reports claimed Taylor was trying to hide her new romance with him from her mum.

A friend told the *National Enquirer*: 'Taylor is actually pretending not to be interested in Cory so her mother doesn't scare him off. Taylor's figured out she better not have any serious mother-daughter conversations about her love life or the relationship will be doomed from the get-go. Taylor really likes Cory, and she's telling friends she sees "real romantic possibilities" with him.'

The couple were then seen having dinner at a deli and getting close at a pre-Grammy party but Cory insisted they were 'just friends'. Later, it was rumoured that he was the inspiration for *Speak Now*'s 'Mine', about a guy that she had a crush on, even though the hidden word in the CD was 'Toby' – the handsome guy who starred in the video.

Increasingly, magazines and gossip sites would speculate about Taylor's love life but she declared herself a 'girl's girl' and clearly both these *Glee* stars were just friends.

She told *InStyle* magazine: 'I have guy friends but the problem with having guy friends is, like, I always get linked to them and they'll end up in a slideshow of people I've apparently dated on the Internet. I mean, there's all kinds of complicated things with having guys as friends. If they have a girlfriend who doesn't like you or things like that. So I have, like, two or three guy friends. A select few. But I have, like, 20–25 really good girlfriends.'

How Taylor found time to socialise at all is quite incredible, as preparations and rehearsals for her tour were all-encompassing.

The show was a monumental display, which saw the artist have nine costume changes and involved 130 people travelling in 21 trucks and 13 buses from city to city. There were 350 lights, 116 speakers and a total of 62 tonnes of equipment hung above the stage from the rafters of the arenas. Highlights of the presentation included the sweeping staircase that led to a raised balcony, church pews, a brilliantly lit tree with a bench, and the Juliet balcony on to which Taylor would enter at the end of each show and fly around the circumference of each arena.

The artist revealed she was inspired by stage shows and her love of theatre, telling her audience: 'The first time that I fell in love with performing was when I went to go and see theatre in my hometown in Pennsylvania. I would see it done incredibly well – going to see Broadway plays of *Wicked* – things like that really inspired me from an early age to love putting on a theatrical performance where there are storylines and characters, and you're always seeing a scene change into another scene. I love telling a story in any way possible.'

She added: 'We spent months going over the set list and thinking where things would go, which ones would segue well into other songs and how we could tell individual stories. I didn't want to tell one big story. I wanted each song to have its own story.'

Taylor also played a total of nine instruments for each show, including several six-string acoustic guitars, an electric guitar, a banjo, a ukulele and a piano. Other highlights included a fake wedding during 'Speak Now', Taylor playing a white grand piano with a twinkling winter snowstorm backdrop for 'Back to December' and fireworks exploding in a riot of colour during 'Dear John'.

Again, she performed various covers: everyone from MGMT and Guns N' Roses, to Joni Mitchell, Coldplay and Alanis Morissette. No two shows were the same.

She kicked off her tour in Asia, travelling to Hong Kong, Taiwan, South Korea, Indonesia and the Philippines, and posted pictures of her and her bandmates dressed as geisha girls. She described her success in Asia as the 'most beautiful and pleasant surprise'.

On stage, she said: 'Being welcomed by countries that speak a different language from the language I speak is an honour. It really touches me every time I look down and I see all the fans singing the words to my songs, having written the lyrics, knowing that they connect in countries where English really isn't spoken by everyone. It means the world to me.'

After the Asia leg of her tour, she travelled to Europe during March, starting in Brussels, before commencing the North American leg in May. She even opened up her dress rehearsal to the public as part of her 'Speak Now . . . Help Now' event, raising money for people affected by the tornadoes that ripped through the south of the country. This part of the tour in America would see her on the road continuously for six months, only missing a few days after getting bronchitis. Unsurprisingly, the critics went crazy for it.

Billboard said: 'Swift's two-hour production was an overwhelming experience. There's an enormous amount of detail that worked to make the Speak Now tour a sort of next step in country concert presentation . . . it blended the pacing, the music and the artist's personality in a way that transfixed,' while the *New York Times* claimed the tour 'went off, as did every number, with clockwork professionalism and thousands of voices singing along and screaming between the lines. Ms. Swift, 22, is their superstar . . . her songs are taut, tuneful narratives.'

Taylor changed the mood of the night up depending on where she was. During the North American leg of the tour, she wrote different song lyrics on her left arm, depending on her disposition.

She told website Taste of Country: 'I have written lyrics on my arm for the last tour, and it was really a fun thing to do because it could be a song I'd never heard before . . . It could be a song that somebody said, "Oh, here, I really like this one line in this one song," you know, in the dressing room before I'd go on, and I'd just write it on my arm!'

Her etchings included: 'You've got every right to a beautiful life', one of her good friend Selena Gomez's lyrics; 'I recommend getting your heart trampled to anybody', from Alanis Morissette's 'You Learn'; and 'It took a while to understand the beauty of letting go', from the Dixie Chicks' 'Let Him Fly'.

During her shows, she also played spontaneous cover versions of songs and paid tributes to home-grown artists, tackling everyone from Bruce Springsteen, the Beach Boys and the Jackson Five to Britney Spears, Fall Out Boy and Eminem. She clearly has friends in high places and also invited some of her musician friends, including Tim McGraw, Jack Ingram, Kenny Chesney, Usher, Nicki Minaj and Justin Bieber to duet with her.

She told the *Tennessean*: 'What I'll do is I'll look forward, really forward in my schedule. The first time it really happened was when I saw that we had four shows in LA. I have a lot of friends in LA, and I wanted to give every single crowd that came to see us over four nights a very different experience.

'It started out with, I really wanted Nicki Minaj to come out. I knew the VMAs were the same week. I really wanted to sing "Super Bass" with Nicki Minaj. For the last year, it's been like my top dream. And so I just got her number and called her and we worked it out. She was so kind to come straight from the VMAs right to our show. It was just magical how that happened.

'And then my friends have a band called Hot Chelle Rae that are doing really well right now, and they happened to be in town, so I invited them for a night, and then Jason Mraz sings one of my favorite songs in the world called "I'm Yours". He lives in LA, so I invited him out for one night. The last-minute one was when Justin Bieber called me the day of the show, and said, "Hey, I'd love to come out."'

During her final gig in North America, at Madison Square Garden in New York at the end of November, Taylor added her own sprinkling of fairy dust to the proceedings. She surprised the packed-out crowd by introducing a special guest to the stage.

'On special occasions, you want to be surrounded by your friends,' she teased. 'And one of my best friends, she is such an amazing singer. We, in the four years of being best friends, have never sung on stage together, and I think that is just such a shame. So it just so happens . . . it just so happens Selena's here tonight.'

As the venue shook with screams, Selena Gomez took to the stage to perform her song 'Who Says', while Taylor accompanied her.

Then, as if the audience were not excited enough, she sat on the sofa in the centre of the stage and recalled her days at school during music class when they would sing James Taylor's 'Fire and Rain' – she labelled it 'probably one of the most fantastic, amazing songs I've ever heard in my life'.

She continued: 'The funny thing about playing Madison Square Garden is that magical, magical things can happen. You never know if James Taylor might just walk out on stage.' With that, the five-time Grammy-winner and Taylor's namesake took to the stage and sang with her.

He later said: 'We just hit it off. I loved her songs, and her presence on stage was so great ... When she called and asked if I would join her at the end of the last tour to celebrate the end of a successful tour on her part, I jumped in.'

On 7 March 2011, her album's third, banjo-laden single, 'Mean', hit the airwaves. It became her thirteenth consecutive hit to be a *Billboard* Country chart Top 10. Many pointed out that the song was about Bob Lefsetz, with words that implied she could see him years down the line in a bar ranting and being bitter, but nobody would be listening. The video broadened the song's message to be about kids at school who are bullied, but it was clear the message was a personal one.

Speaking to *Parade* magazine, she elaborated: 'Some days I'm fine and I can just brush it off and go about my day, but some days it absolutely levels me. All I can do is continue to try to work hard every single day and feel everything. I think it's important for me to feel things because then I write songs about them. The whole idea of being criticised and the fact that that entered my life made for a song that I'm very proud of on the record called "Mean".'

The critics enjoyed her retaliation, with the *Los Angeles Times* declaring: it 'smacks down critics who say she can't sing . . . by declaring that someday she'll be "livin' in a great big city" and they'll be drunk in some dive bar, bloviating into the void.'

She also used the song to inform her charity work and told

Seventeen that her parents taught her 'never to judge others based on whom they love, what colour their skin is or their religion'. Taylor has always opposed LGBT discrimination and the video dealt with homophobia in school, when a boy is bullied for reading a fashion magazine in a locker room; he later turns out to become a famous fashion designer.

Taylor said: 'Why make life miserable for someone when you could be using your energy for good? We don't need to share the same opinions as others, but we need to be respectful. When you hear people making hateful comments, stand up to them. Point out what a waste it is to hate, and you could open their eyes.'

Her words seemed to reach out and touch so many groups of people. The *New York Times* said Taylor was part of 'a new wave of young (and mostly straight) women who are providing the soundtrack for a generation of gay fans coming to terms with their identity in a time of turbulent and confusing cultural messages'.

On 2 April, she performed the single at the Academy of Country Music (ACM) Awards in Las Vegas. Wearing a gold Grecian-style dress, Taylor was a big winner on the night picking up the prestigious Entertainer of the Year gong. She covered her mouth with her hands, did a little dance and hugged Brad Paisley and Miranda Lambert on the way to the stage after winning the fan-voted award, the only major ACM award determined by popular vote.

She said: 'This is the first time that I've ever won this and I'm just losing my mind. The fact that this is from the fans makes it so beautiful.'

She also picked up Top Album Artist and Top Country Artist at the *Billboard* Music Awards. Turning heads in a sparkling Ellie Saab gown, Taylor said: 'I'm just having the best time doing this.'

On 19 April, 'The Story of Us' was released as the fourth single spawned from *Speak Now*, while 'Sparks Fly', the fifth single, was released on 18 July.

Taylor had written 'Sparks Fly' when she was sixteen and it had grown in popularity among her fan base since she first played it live, in 2007. She was right to release it as a single as it catapulted straight to the top of the country chart. It also debuted at No. 17 on the *Billboard* Hot 100 to strong digital sales of 113,000 downloads. It was one of the songs that made Taylor the first act to have ten songs debut on the *Billboard* Hot 100 in the same week.

The awards just kept stacking up. In August, she won a total of six gongs at the Teen Choice Awards: Choice Music Female Artist, Choice Music Female Country Artist, Choice Red Carpet Fashion Icon Female, Choice Music Country Single for 'Mean' and Choice Music Breakup Song for 'Back to December'. Channelling Marilyn Monroe, in a short cream dress, she danced in the audience and sang along as her friend Selena Gomez performed 'Love You Like a Love Song'.

The crooner was also honoured for her contributions to entertainment with the Ultimate Choice Award, the show's version of a lifetime achievement award, which had previously been won by Justin Timberlake, Britney Spears and Reese Witherspoon. Accepting her Ultimate Teen Choice surfboard on stage, she thanked her fans and joked: 'It's been a long time since I was a teenager, like two years.'

Although it was a joke, Taylor vocalised just how much she had achieved in a short space of time. She had an intrinsic connection to her fans and reached out to them in the remainder of her speech. She noted how teenagers often are teased by adults because they are 'intense' or 'romantic', but she encouraged kids in the audience and watching at home on the Fox TV network, saying: 'I think all those things are amazing things, and to all the teens watching, I hope you never lose those things.'

While she was on the road, her own scent, Wonderstruck, was released as part of a deal with renowned perfumer Elizabeth Arden. With her red lipstick, chic hairstyle and pretty striped dress, she looked the picture of sophisticated glamour at the launch at Macy's department store in New York.

'It says: "I'm wonderstruck, blushing all the way home,"' she said to *Good Morning America*. 'I've always loved that line and the phrase "wonderstruck". I don't hear it very often.'

Perhaps hoping to appeal to her broad fan base, the star said she had designed the perfume for 'people of all ages', but admitted she has had to 'talk some of my guy friends out of wearing it. So it's debatable whether it's, you know, for both [sexes].' She also compared the effect of perfume with music, saying: 'Fragrance has a lot to do with shaping people's memories in the way that music does.'

Companies were falling over themselves to sign Taylor up

to promote their products. Among other things, she has sold a Walmart line of $14 sundresses, along with calendars, iPad skins, robes, journals, gift bags and headbands; she has been a spokesperson for Sony Cyber-shot digital cameras; and she has created a greetings cards line for American Greetings Corporation, because she was writing so many notes every week.

'Part of the reason I wanted to do it was because I go through so many cards on a weekly basis,' she told the *New York Times*. 'I like writing 'em. And I like stamps.'

By around November 2011, the Speak Now tour had been going for the best part of a year, playing back-to-back shows, and Taylor was worked ragged but she said she wouldn't have it any other way.

In an interview with the *Tennessean*, she said: 'Actually, I don't know what I'm going to do when I'm not on this tour anymore. I think I'm so in love with this tour that I just love being on it. I love being part of it. I love the schedule. I love the crowds. I love the feeling you get when you walk off stage and it was a good show.'

However, she also revealed that she had been writing and was already looking towards her next album.

'Of course I'll move on to the next thing after this tour's over,' she explained. 'And that will probably be overdrive recording and obsessing over my next album. The whole thing kind of works naturally in a two-year phase. When you're creating an album for two years and you're finally ready to put it out, it's all you think about. Hopefully, we'll get there, and there will be plenty to do at the end of this tour. There will be plenty to plan for.'

She also explained to MTV that she wanted it to be perfect.

'So far, I've been writing so much in the last year and my label keeps telling me, "All right, we're finished; all right, we're satisfied; okay, this is done now." And then I just keep writing and I keep turning it in in different versions.'

Speaking about the theme of the next hit, she explained: 'I think that love is always going to be a huge theme in what I write about just because there are no two similar relationships, there are no two times that you feel love the same way or hurt the same way or [feel] rejection the same way. It's all different and I'm fascinated by that ... As you grow, you change in the way you process emotion.'

The emotions she felt when she continued to receive recognition from the music industry were always the same: awestruck jubilation.

On 10 November 2011, Taylor attended the CMAs in Nashville and gave a stripped-back acoustic performance of 'Ours', which she released later that month as the sixth and final single from the album; it also became her third No. 1. She was dressed in a casual pink jumper and sat on a sofa, which was a far cry from her normal glittering, all-out performances.

Back in her gorgeous oyster gown, she walked away with her second Entertainer of the Year Award. Helped with a crib sheet on her arm of who to thank, she spoke about how much she was looking forward to her next album, saying:

'With this next album I'm so excited because I've been writing so much. We're still in the first gear of making it, so as we finish songs and demo them in my producer's basement, I can picture them being played on the stage. One of the things I love about the Speak Now tour is that it's very theatrical and each song has its own treatment. The reason I obsess over it so much is that I obsess over writing them so much.'

She also took the opportunity to thank her entourage, recognising that without them, her huge success wouldn't be possible.

'The reason why we celebrate like we just won the Super Bowl is that my band and crew, the dancers, the aerialists, the catering crew, my family, friends and fans all over the world were paying attention tonight and they were excited because they're part of this.'

With her trophy cabinet bursting at the seams, no doubt, she also went on to pick up an American Music Award for Favorite Country Album for *Speak Now*, Favorite Country Female Artist and – the top prize – Artist of the Year.

'This is so crazy!' the superstar said after she beat contenders such as Adele, Lady Gaga and Katy Perry to capture all three awards.

Life on the road must have been tough – and lonely – for the young star, so in November she added a new member to her entourage: a tiny Scottish Fold kitten, Meredith.

'Hanging out with my new roommate Meredith,' she tweeted along with an Instagram picture of the fluffy moggy. The picture got thousands of 'likes' and Katy Perry even tweeted her back, saying: 'OH MY GOSH. Is this kitty for real?!?!' Taylor answered saying she was chasing her own tail.

Taylor, who also has two Dobermans, Bug and Baby, later explained her name to *Us Weekly*, saying 'Her name is Meredith – Meredith Grey because she's a gray cat, and because I love *Grey's Anatomy* . . . She's awesome. She's like one of those cats that give cats a good name. She doesn't hide under furniture and get weird around people. She's really friendly and fun and she's perfect for the road because she doesn't ever get freaked out. So I'm really glad that she has a cool personality.'

In her time off from the show, she said she had TV marathons watching her favourite crime shows, *CSI* and *Law & Order*.

Her momentum just never seemed to slow. In December she unveiled 'Safe & Sound', a collaboration with The Civil Wars for *The Hunger Games* soundtrack.

'Something I've been VERY excited about for a VERY long time is going to be happening VERY soon,' she tweeted, teasing her followers and adding, 'and I'm not referring to Christmas.' She then added: 'And this is it, the big surprise . . . Go get it! #TheHungerGames', with a link to the song's album art.

Within minutes #safeandsound became the top trending topic on Twitter in the USA and the second hottest topic worldwide.

The year ended with Taylor being named as *Billboard*'s prestigious Woman of the Year. Bill Werde, *Billboard*'s Editorial Director, said: 'Taylor has shown the power of good songwriting with music that has transcended genres, and we're thrilled to recognize all of her successes over the past year by honouring her with the *Billboard* Woman of the Year Award. At the young age of 21, Taylor has already made a major impact on music and has been an incredible role model for aspiring singers/songwriters and young women everywhere. I look forward to watching her career continue to flourish in the years to come.'

But if anyone thought another immense year had changed the singer, they were wrong. Talking about her Christmas wish list to *People* magazine, she said: '[My list] includes a pasta maker, antique picture frames and anything from Free People or Anthropologie.'

In a message to her fans, she added: 'I hope that they're happy, wherever they are . . . [that] they feel loved by the people around them. . . And most of all I hope they feel appreciated by me. My life would look nothing like this without them.'

Everyone wanted to see Taylor happy with a new man and before long the media were hooking her up again. The 22-year-old was spotted enjoying a flirtatious dinner with Zac Efron, according to *Us Weekly* magazine. The superstar duo allegedly arrived at an Italian restaurant together in Zac's car and 'were deep in conversation and very giggly', according to the magazine's source.

Zac, who is two years Taylor's senior, had been single since splitting from his *High School Musical* co-star Vanessa Hudgens in December 2010, and had said that she was a 'lovely girl, very beautiful', while Taylor returned the favour, branding Zac an 'all-around amazing guy'.

The gossip was soon shot down when an insider claimed that the two are just good friends. 'They were in LA doing press stuff together, and after they were done, they decided to grab dinner,' they said; while another informant added: 'Taylor thinks Zac's cute ... [but] they are on totally different wavelengths.'

She was also linked to British actor Eddie Redmayne after she met him at an audition for the big-screen version of *Les Misérables* the previous October. 'They hung out in New York City with the movie's execs,' a source told *Us Weekly*. 'And Taylor developed feelings for him fast.'

The pair were then said to have kept in touch after Eddie returned to the UK and met up briefly again in London in January but after returning to the UK Taylor found that she had lost out to West End star Samantha Barks for the role of Eponine and the romance floundered.

'Taylor loved this image of a British boyfriend,' the source added. 'But Eddie's not interested in a long-distance relationship. The elements were against them. It's a shame.'

However, the actor later denied they were ever an item and said it was 'absolute nonsense', telling the *Daily Telegraph*: 'We had a chat behind the stage for seven minutes. So I met Taylor Swift for an hour and seven minutes. Even by my standards that's a pretty brief relationship.'

Eddie had homed in on one very important detail: the lack of time for a relationship.

During January, Taylor made her debut appearance on the

front cover of fashion bible *Vogue* and she opened up about her love life, saying: 'I got nothing going on. I just don't really feel like dating.'

However, she did declare that her fourth album would document more heartache. 'There's just been this earth-shattering, not recent, but absolute crash-and-burn heartbreak,' she told the magazine. 'And that will turn out to be what the next album is about.'

She continued: 'I think I am smart unless I am really, really in love, and then I am ridiculously stupid'; and explained she had learned a few things from her failed relationships: 'I have a few red flags now. If someone doesn't seem to want to get to know me as a person but instead seems to have kind of bought into the whole idea of me and he approves of my Wikipedia page [along with] men who are threatened by what I do.'

In February she was recognised again at the Grammy Awards, where her track 'Mean' netted her Best Country Solo Performance and Best Country Song.

'There is no feeling quite like writing a song about someone who is mean to you and makes your life miserable and winning a Grammy for it,' she said, while accepting the trophy. 'Thank you.'

She was wearing a nude silk gown by Zuhair Murad, Prada shoes and a chic up 'do, but changed into a vintage floral dress and brown lace-up shoes for a performance of the winning track. Taking her set back to the Depression era and joined by a bluegrass band, Taylor strummed an electric banjo guitar bearing her lucky number 13 on the front. The instrument also had the words 'Someday . . . I'll be big enough so you can't hit me' scrawled across the front, lyrics from her song. Having written the song in response to harsh criticism, Taylor changed up the last lines to say, 'Someday, I'll be singing this at the Grammys.'

Her performance received a standing ovation from her fellow artists and *Time* magazine noted: 'The tune is a direct response to a critic who attacked her (undeniably terrible) 2010 Grammy performance with Stevie Nicks, in which Swift seemed to sing off-key. Tonight, Swift delivered her comeback on-key and with a vengeance . . . OK, Taylor. This is a great song, and you're younger, cuter and more talented than any professional critic who has ever cut you down. You win.'

USA Today also noted: 'It would seem that the experience made her a better songwriter and live performer.'

As Taylor knew all too well: revenge was sweet.

CHAPTER TEN

'I haven't heard from him since. I think I was just insistent enough this time'

When Taylor was a little girl sitting in her bedroom scribbling poems in her notebook, she tried to emulate one of her favourite childhood poets, Dr Seuss, who is famed for works like *The Cat in the Hat* and *How the Grinch Stole Christmas*. In March 2012, she made an appearance in a colourful animated version of Seuss's *The Lorax*, where she voiced the character of tree-loving Audrey, the love interest of Ted, an idealistic young boy, played by Zac Efron.

'Dr Seuss books were a huge, huge part of my childhood and it really made me fall in love with the way you can make words bounce off a page if you get them in the right syncopation,' she explained.

Talking to MTV about the differences between her music

and voiceover work, she dished: 'It's a completely different space that you go to in your head. It's very different from when you're singing songs that you wrote ... With this, you're sitting there in a booth by yourself having conversations with no one.'

Having scripted conversations by yourself might seem like a lonely gig, but Taylor loved the earthy character.

'She's heavenly,' she explained. 'She's such a daydreamer, and she cares so much about the past. To some degree, you have to have a priority based on the past and the future as well as the present.'

To promote the film Taylor and Zac embarked on an Ellen DeGeneres inspired 'dance-dare' on the orange carpet at the Hollywood premiere, where they boogied along to LMFAO's 'Sexy and I Know It'.

Much to his embarrassment, Zac was also seen to drop a condom on the carpet by mistake, but if some sneaky loving post-premiere was on the cards for Zac, it certainly wasn't with Taylor.

Talking about her Valentine's Day plans on *The Ellen DeGeneres Show* the same week, she said: 'I actually had a pathetic single girl's party – it was cool! That's actually what it was called. I'm not saying being single is pathetic – because we've talked about this, I think being single is awesome – but I had all my single girlfriends over and we ate junk food ... and danced and made these little profile cards about why we were single.'

She and Zac also took the opportunity to set the record straight about their relationship:

'We are not a couple,' Taylor elaborated. 'He's awesome; we are not a couple though. You hear people get together when they're shooting movies, co-stars. But not, like, animated co-stars – you know what I'm saying? Oh, my God, as we were recording our voiceovers on separate coasts, we really connected.'

They did perform a duet together on the show, and Zac said to CMT that Taylor had taught him to play the guitar – and was a brilliant tutor:

'She's a great teacher. In the past, everyone who's tried to teach me guitar starts with music theory and stuff like that. I tend to just doze off after a while. She went straight into songs. She taught me, like, four chords and I'm already playing all the good campfire songs.'

Taylor used the buzz around the film to advocate reading for young children and donated thousands of books to schools and libraries, including 14,000 copies to the Nashville Public Library, which was off the back of a $250,000 donation to help schools she had attended buy books and fun educational programmes. She loved to encourage children to read; it was a cause very close to her heart. She co-chaired the National Education Association's Read Across America campaign and recorded a message encouraging children to pick up books.

With her big screen debut done and dusted, rumours gathered pace that her next role would be Joni Mitchell in a film adaptation of Sheila Weller's 2008 book *Girls Like Us*, which chronicled the lives of Mitchell, Carly Simon and Carole King and how they reshaped American music.

However, she later revealed to *Time* that nothing was set in stone and clearly many scripts had made their way into her hands.

'That's actually not confirmed,' she said. 'I wish I could say it's confirmed! But the thing about movies that I've learned is – I've been reading scripts for five years, and you just don't know what ones are going to get greenlit and which ones aren't, so I can't talk about it unless it's the real thing.'

However, she may well take on more acting roles in the future, enthusiastically adding: 'I would love to sign on to do a movie if it was the right role and if it was the right script, because I would be taking time away from music to tell a big grand story, and spend all of my time and pouring all of my emotions into being someone else. So for me to do that, it would have to be a story worth telling.'

In March, she was back on the road for the Australasian leg of her Speak Now tour and the timing was perfect: the crowds and the critics adored her. The *Sunday Times* in Perth called it 'dazzling', Adelaide Now website declared the starlet 'delighted the crowd' and the *New Zealand Herald* added, after wrapping her final date in Auckland: 'We're unlikely to witness a show like that again in a long, long time. Maybe ever.'

She graced the cover of Australia's *Harper's Bazaar* magazine and, showing there were no hard feelings between her and Kanye West, she even modelled a top from his fashion collection, which had been universally panned. On the front, she channelled the Roaring Twenties in a Gucci flapper dress, looking chic.

Taylor's style had evolved from teen girl with messy blonde curls to mature fashionista pulling off sophisticated designer looks on the red carpet with ease. Throughout, she has remained ultra-feminine and girly – by her own admission, she is still 'like, totally a dress girl'. She has also called herself 'experimental' and in the past two years she has morphed into a fashion leader, often sticking to sequins and glitter.

'I'm inspired by retro styles throughout history,' she added, to website iVillage. 'I love red lips and vintage hairstyles. I try to be pretty open-minded about fashion, but I always end up coming back to feminine things that usually sparkle.'

She was becoming quite a fashion icon with designers clamouring to dress her for the constant merry-go-round of the awards ceremonies and her name appearing on best-dressed lists all over the world.

However, she has never wanted her image to become more important than her music, telling *Vogue*: 'I don't ever want to be that person whose self-image overtakes who they are.'

She has always been naturally blessed with a long, slim figure and insists she doesn't work out.

'There's no regimen. There's no personal trainer,' she maintained. 'I love to go hiking because it's an experience.'

She has always said she will never take her clothes off for sexier shoots.

'It's just a life decision,' she told the *Daily Telegraph*. 'I like wearing pretty dresses and I like trying out new styles but I don't feel comfortable taking my clothes off. I wouldn't wear tiny amounts of clothing in my real life so I don't think it's necessary to wear that stuff in photo-shoots.'

Taylor would never need to do anything like taking her clothes of to gain publicity. On her return to the USA in March, she enjoyed a weekend that was pretty incredible, even by her standards.

First, at Los Angeles' USC Galen Center, she was handed the Nickelodeon Kids' Choice Big Help Award for her charity work by none other than the US President's wife, the First Lady, Michelle Obama, who was attending the event with her two daughters, Malia and Sasha.

Taylor never shouts about it, but a lot of her spare time is spent helping charities. Donations by the star have included $75,000 to Hendersonville High School to help refurbish the school's auditorium, $60,000 to textbook rental company Chegg to help the music departments in six colleges and a staggering $4 million she has pledged to fund the building of an education centre at the Country Music Hall of Fame and Museum in Nashville, which is scheduled to open in 2014 and where Taylor will be involved in an advisory capacity.

Her list of donations to charities helping sick children is endless and, during her rare time off, she goes to many hospitals to visit the youngsters and often donates auctionable items to charities such as the Elton John AIDS Foundation, UNICEF and Oxfam.

'Taylor Swift may be in the news most often for her award-winning songs and multi-platinum records, but every step of the way she has always made it a point to give back,' the First Lady said from the stage. 'She's supported children's charities, she's worked to combat bullying, and given over tens of thousands of books to schools and libraries all around the country.'

But despite Taylor's own stardom, the pop singer was starstruck when she took the stage to meet her idol, who was dressed for the event in skinny metallic jeans and a v-neck top.

'I've always wanted to meet you! This is amazing. I'm so honoured to get . . . to be receiving this award from the First Lady of the United States – I am freaking out.'

Then before she had time to even take in this huge tribute, the following night she was out again at the annual Academy of Country Music Awards, where she dazzled in a slim-fitting J. Mendel dress paired with smoky eye make-up. For the second straight year, the industry darling won the prestigious Entertainer of the Year accolade, in a race where she was the only female.

'I want to say to my fellow nominees in this category, I respect you so much and I love you,' she said to Kenny Chesney, Jason Aldean, Brad Paisley and Blake Shelton. 'To the fans for voting, thank you for doing this. This is exciting. Thank you!'

The evening was slightly tempered with melancholy because she had promised a young fan Kevin McGuire, who had cancer, that he could be her date for the night but he was ill and unable to attend. 'He's not here but I promised I would give him a shout-out,' Taylor said.

The singer had first learned of the New Jersey teen when his sister Victoria made a Facebook page asking Taylor to be his date to the prom. While she was unable to make it to his prom, she offered an alternative.

'Kevin, I'm so sorry but I won't be able to make it to your prom. But I was wondering, the ACM Awards are coming up . . . Would you be my date? Love, Taylor,' she posted.

The songstress had arranged to fly Kevin and his family out to Las Vegas for the event, and set up their hotel accommodation, as well as his tuxedo and shoes.

Unfortunately, the twenty-five hours of chemotherapy that he went through was too much for his system to take. In spite of the hiccup Taylor promised him that they would have their date and he joked: 'How many people can say they turned down Taylor Swift?'

Just weeks later, the kind-hearted singer also made a personal phone call and sent flowers to the family of Sergeant Wade Wilson, who died during combat in Afghanistan. Sergeant Wilson's comrades made a YouTube video plea to the star, inviting her to the marine's funeral because he was such a big fan, and she told his family that she would like to wear his dog tags in her next video to show her support for his military service.

Multitasking is clearly one of the singer's strengths but, at the end of April, Taylor finally had some proper time relaxing back at her home in LA. The previous year she had invested her hard-earned money in a new $3.5 million pad in Beverly Hills. The four-bedroom, four-bathroom home – described by the star as 'cosy, Anthropologie, grandma chic' – is set on an exclusive 1.5-acre estate in the Santa Monica mountains. It is understood that she bought it so she didn't have to spend time in hotels. Not long before, she had also splashed out on a $1.4-million historic redbrick mansion for her family, with four bedrooms, five bathrooms, hardwood floors and a walled garden for privacy.

Clearly, Taylor had taken the advice of her father on board and was investing her money wisely. She certainly had plenty to invest. In May, *Forbes* named her as the highest-paid celebrity under thirty, beating Justin Bieber and Rihanna, with earnings in the previous twelve months topping $57 million.

During her time in LA, she caught up with her friends. One night, she was seen dressed in a skin-tight catsuit for her actress friend Dianna Agron's twenty-sixth birthday party, complete with matching ears, whiskers and a racy studded collar. The star posted a picture of herself and her friends on Instagram, with the caption: 'The most magical night at @DiannaAgron's circus-themed birthday party.'

It was the second time that week Taylor had played dress up with her pals. She was seen alongside her friends celebrating the birthday of US actress Shirley MacLaine. In ladylike hats, dainty gloves and 1950s-style lacy dresses, the girls visited the elite Beverly Hills Hotel and dined at the hotel's famed Polo Lounge. They even ordered a special dessert in honour of MacLaine, who had turned seventy-eight years old.

'We dressed up full-time fancy and went out in celebration of Shirley MacLaine's birthday,' Taylor wrote in an accompanying tweet.

On another date, she posted pictures of an evening where they painted each other's faces and Taylor sported an impressive blue-and-black butterfly on her cheek and forehead. 'Evidently, it was "face paint Wednesday" last night,' she wrote.

Taylor and Diana were also seen dining out together in matching floral dresses at Dominick's restaurant in West Hollywood and the *Glee* star later joked on the Jimmy Kemmel show that they were dating. When the host asked: 'Are you dating her? That would be great,' the actress, who plays Quinn Fabray on the hit show, replied: 'Wouldn't that be juicy?' before turning to the camera, blowing a kiss and purring, 'Hi, Taylor.'

Taylor was seen having a girly gossip with Selena Gomez on a couple of occasions but she also had some time to herself, and she enjoys her own company.

'I go home and I watch TV and I sit there, with my cat, and I just watch TV or go online, check my emails,' she said to Taste of Country. 'It's nice to just light a candle next to your bed and like . . . no one's around.'

She also cooks for her friends and has impromptu sing-along sessions.

'My favourite thing is getting to have my friends over and cook for them,' she said. 'Hanging out with friends at home always turns into some piano singalong, so I have all kinds of percussion instruments and guitars lying around.'

These quiet evenings at home are always cherished by the star who spends as many nights on stage and at award shows as she does relaxing. At the end of May, she attended the *Billboard* Music Awards, to pick up her prize in person for Woman of the Year, and looked incredible in a vampish-red dress by Ellie Saab.

Before she took the stage, singer Kris Kristofferson paid tribute to her, while the audience were treated to a montage of moments from her phenomenally successful career so far. *New Girl* actress Zooey Deschanel then presented the award to Taylor, who was quick to thank her fans for their support.

She said: 'Thanks to so many people, but mostly my family, everyone who's helped me get here and the fans. I just love you so much. I am so humbled and honoured by this. And thank you to Kris Kristofferson and Zooey Deschanel for coming out here for this – that was so nice. *Billboard*, thank you for everything you've done for me, all the fans, I just love you.'

In August, she had another blinding night at the Teen Choice Awards, where she bagged five gongs, including the prestigious Choice Female Artist. She was also one of the biggest victors in the fashion stakes and rocked a white back-less dress by Maria Lucia Hohan, teamed with Prada peep-toe nude heels, on the hot-pink carpet. As well as the top prize, she also won nods for Choice Female Country Artist, Choice Single by a Female Artist for 'Eyes Open', Choice Country Song for 'Sparks Fly' and Choice Movie Voice for her performance as Audrey in *The Lorax*.

She was particularly excited about the latter award, telling *Access Hollywood*: 'I was so excited about that because you know when you hear your voice played back on a voicemail and you're like, "Oh, my god. Is that what I sound like?" So to get an award for your voice is cool.'

Afterwards, she tweeted: '5 Teen Choice Awards?! I'm so happy I'm so happy I'm so happy I'm so happy I'm so happy – thank you so much for voting!'

By then, Taylor was pop royalty so it was appropriate that she spent the Thanksgiving holiday at the legendary family home of the Kennedys – 'America's royal family' – in Hyannis Port in Massachusetts. The family's legacy is entrenched in politics and celebrity, the most prominent being President John F. Kennedy. In addition to fame and political power, the Kennedy clan have had more than their fair share of tragedy and several members of the family have died in assassinations and accidents, in what's called 'the Kennedy curse'.

The waterfront property in Cape Cod has served as a backdrop for many of the family gatherings over the years and during this sunny weekend, the young singer was seen boating and relaxing in the sun with members of the Kennedy clan and Arnold Schwarzenegger's 18-year-old son, Patrick, whose mum Maria Shriver is part of the dynasty.

Taylor has always been open about her fixation with the family, telling one magazine: 'I'm just so obsessed with the whole history of JFK and RFK,' adding that she had completed a 900-page book called *The Kennedy Women*.

She became acquainted with the Kennedys after the

singer attended the red-carpet premiere of *Ethel*, an HBO documentary about the life of Ethel Kennedy, earlier in the year. She admitted that she was 'starstruck' after meeting Caroline and Ethel Kennedy, and began to get friendly with the family soon after.

'I got to spend the afternoon with Ethel a couple of weeks ago,' she told *Vogue* at the time. 'She is one of my favourites, because you look back at the pictures of her and Bobby and they always look like they are having the most fun out of everybody. You know, eleven kids, all these exotic animals on their property. I've read a lot about them.'

While Taylor was originally linked with Patrick, it soon became apparent that the object of her attention wasn't the film actor's son but Conor Kennedy, JFK's great nephew. At eighteen years old at the time, he was four years Taylor's junior, but the couple didn't let the age gap hold them back and were seen kissing and holding hands during a romantic weekend together a few weeks later. It was reported that Ethel had decided to play Cupid after bringing them together at the family's gated home for the holiday weekend.

During a press tour, she was quizzed about Taylor one day becoming a member of the iconic political dynasty and gushed: 'We should be so lucky.'

Her daughter Rory added: '[Taylor] is a great friend of all of ours. We love her. She's awesome.'

Two weeks later, Taylor and Conor were seen at the Kennedy house again, going to a house party before joining some friends at a local pizza restaurant. The following day, the singer did face painting with some of the children, and later she and Conor were spotted reading books together on Ethel's lawn. Apparently, the Kennedy heir, whose mother Mary Richardson Kennedy had committed suicide earlier in the year, had fallen hard for Taylor.

A source told the *New York Times*: 'I was a little surprised. It's been two weeks and he's in love. He thinks of her as his girlfriend – not just friends or dating. He calls her his girlfriend.'

The romance seemed to be gathering pace when Taylor took Conor home to Nashville to meet her parents for dinner. Excited fans posted pictures of the couple on Twitter as the pair visited Starbucks, Pancake Pantry and various other cafes in Taylor's local town.

Throughout the summer, the couple were pictured around Cape Cod and Nantucket, embracing and kissing with abandon. On one occasion, Taylor was paddling in the sea, hand in hand with Conor, before they kicked a football around in front of the Kennedys' home. She rocked old-school glamour, modelling a selection of different-style polka-dot swimsuits, along with her signature red lippy. Taylor was said to be helping Conor deal with the heartbreak of losing his mother and was encouraging him to take his mind off it by pursuing his interest in whale research.

An insider told the *New York Post*: 'Taylor has a really generous and positive spirit, and the whole Kennedy family loves her. It has been a very difficult time for Conor, losing his mother, and Taylor has great positive energy. She is definitely helping him through this.'

When Taylor was forced back to New York because of

work commitments, she reportedly sent her private jet to pick Conor up because she felt so lost without him.

'Taylor missed Conor so much, she sent a plane for him a few days later,' a source told the *Post*'s Page Six. 'He's been with her ever since, and his family doesn't know when he will be back. Things have become so serious between them so fast that no one in Hyannis Port would be surprised if they eloped.'

Taylor had first purchased her own private 12-seater jet back in 2011, costing a reported $40 million, and had her lucky number 13 painted on its nose.

Around this time it was claimed that Taylor was enjoying the fruits of her labour and had expanded her property portfolio with a $4.8 million oceanfront mansion in Cape Cod, next door to the Kennedys' house, after she fell in love with the area during her visits to see Conor. The seven-bedroom colonial-style property featured six bathrooms, a private beach and guesthouse, and was on a private road. She sold the property on seven months later for a huge $1million profit.

She was later asked about it but remained coy, telling *Vanity Fair*: 'People say that about me, that I apparently buy houses near every boy I like, that's a thing that I apparently do. If I like you, I will apparently buy up the real estate market just to freak you out so you leave me.'

While things looked great for Taylor on a romance front, her parents' relationship had apparently hit rocky ground and there were reports that Andrea and Scott Swift had split up after almost twenty-five years together. The strain of spending so much time apart became too much but they didn't want to make it official in case it impacted their daughter's reputation.

A source told US magazine, *Star*: 'They haven't filed for a divorce because they don't want it to damage Taylor's career.'

It was claimed they had lived separately for two years and Taylor had, in fact, bought two homes for them to live in back in Nashville, not just one. Taylor's reps refused to comment but the insider added that her new album would 'showcase the pain of her parent's separation'.

Whatever the true story, Taylor went to work as normal. The next big event on her agenda was unveiling her next lead single. On 13 August, she took part in a webchat, which gave fans a first listen to the lead song from album *Red* – which would be released at the end of October. Over 72,500 viewers tuned in to hear the track and ask questions.

Surrounded by a group of devotees who giggled at her every word, the Grammy-winner jokingly introduced the song, entitled 'We Are Never Ever Getting Back Together', saying: 'So this is the new single. It's a really romantic song.' She sarcastically added: 'It's really touching and sensitive . . . for my lovely ex-boyfriend.'

The lyrics to the song paint a relatively straightforward picture that Taylor was messed around by a former flame, although no names are mentioned. After compiling *Speak Now* completely by herself, she had decided to collaborate with other writers for her fourth album.

Talking to *Good Morning America*, she said: 'I think for me this album tended to really explore the edges of what I'm allowed to do. Exploring, kind of pushing myself and taking myself out of my comfort zone which is writing alone and going and working with my heroes; songwriters that have influenced me my whole career. Or really challenged me in the best way possible.'

Co-written by two Swedish songwriters – Max Martin, who has also penned tracks for Britney Spears and Backstreet Boys – and Shellback (the Swedish songwriter Karl Johan Schuster) – who is behind songs by Usher, Pink and Maroon 5 – 'We Are Never Ever Getting Back Together' was more bubblegum pop than ever before.

The song had been born when she was in the studio with the two writers – and a friend of her ex walked in.

'He starts talking about how he's heard we were getting back together and that was not the case,' she said to *Good Morning America*. 'When he leaves, Max and Johan are like, "So what's the story behind that?" And so I start telling them the story of break up, get back together, break up, get back together, just, ugh, the worst.

'Max says, "This is what we're writing. We're writing this song," and I picked up the guitar and just started singing, "We are never".' She continued: 'It just happened so fast. It was so much fun.'

In the webcast, Taylor said she decided to use the title *Red* for the album because 'it was really simple' and epitomised the different emotions she has experienced.

'Thinking about what that means to me and all the different emotions that are written about on this album –

they're all pretty much about the tumultuous, crazy, insane, intense, semi-toxic relationships that I've experienced in the last two years,' she noted. 'All those emotions – spanning from intense love, intense frustration, jealousy, confusion – in my mind, all those emotions are red. There's nothing in between; there is nothing beige about any of those feelings.'

The singer also revealed she had written as many as thirty or thirty-five songs, which she had managed to cut back to sixteen. She added: 'I am so excited for you to hear the new direction of things.'

Everyone wanted to know who 'We Are Never Ever Getting Back Together' was about and the general consensus that the man in question was Jake Gyllenhaal. It was clear after her biting track 'Dear John' that is wasn't John Mayer, and Joe Jonas ruled himself out, telling a radio station: 'I can say it's not about me, because I don't think we've ever tried another time. I can tell you it's not about me. I think we're cool. It's pretty years removed.'

Meanwhile, a source told *Us Weekly*, the anthem was 'definitely about Jake'. Critics pointed out that, in the video, Taylor's boyfriend – played by actor Noah Mills – wears a navy vest, similar to the one the actor sported during one of their dates; that the bracelet Taylor has on looks suspiciously like the one Jake was rumoured to have given her for her birthday; and that her man gives her a scarf, reminiscent of pictures of Taylor wearing Jake's scarf wrapped around her neck. Combined with this was the fact that just days after their split in January the couple were seen having dinner together near Taylor's Nashville flat, sparking rumours that they had reconciled.

During an interview on Spanish TV show *El Hormiguero*, while talking about the single, she revealed that Jake was not 'dependable'.

'I think once a relationship is done it's done, you can't do that back and forth thing – it's the most exhausting process,' Taylor told the host. 'I think you have to have somebody that's dependable, that isn't going to change their mind every five seconds.'

Later, chat-show host Katie Couric asked her whether the subject of her song got the message and Taylor replied: 'I haven't heard from him since. I think I was just insistent enough this time.'

The single was an instant success and within fifty minutes it was at the top of the iTunes chart, breaking a previous record held by Lady Gaga for 'Born This Way'. It was also Taylor's first song to peak at the top of the *Billboard* Hot 100, leaping from No. 72, marking the biggest jump by any artist into the top spot.

Rolling Stone named it as the second best song of 2012, adding: 'It's like a Clash of the Titans: Swift, the world's hottest pop singer *or* songwriter, meets up with Max Martin, the Swedish maestro who's been the Dr. Evil of global trash-disco for more than a decade. To nobody's surprise, they cook up a perfect three-minute teen tantrum about country girls getting mad at high-strung indie boys, topping the charts faster than you can say, "This is exhausting." It's a stadium-chant breakup song that may have less to do with the actual guy it's about than with the massive raging-cowgirl audience Swift has led to the pinnacle of the music world.'

Taylor used the opportunity of her latest single to bring out a new fragrance, Wonderstruck Enchanted, and posed with it, dressed in a bright pink gown.

'I love the look of my ad,' she told *People* magazine. 'I'm wearing this amazing gown that I loved as soon as I put it on. It's a classic look, and that's been my recent style obsession. Anything classic and timeless.'

Describing the scent, which was a sister product to the original, Wonderstruck, she added: 'Wonderstruck Enchanted is the next chapter in the story of my Wonderstruck fragrance. Wonderstruck is about that moment when you instantly feel a connection to someone, but then there's that feeling of being completely enamoured – enchanted – when you know a little more about that someone and still feel that strong connection.'

Her romance with the Kennedy heir was clearly serious. They were next seen during a poignant visit to Conor's mother's grave, where she comforted him and held his hand as he bowed his head in prayer.

Not long after, there were claims that Taylor was asked to leave Conor's cousin Kyle Kennedy's Boston wedding twice by her angry mother Victoria Gifford Kennedy as she was worried the young starlet would take attention away from the bride. Sources claimed that Taylor refused and attended anyway. However, her spokesperson Paula Erikson shot back at the claims and said Taylor was welcomed by all the family and the bride was delighted Taylor was there, and 'thanked her profusely'.

There were also stories that Taylor wanted to take Conor to the romantic destination of Paris at the start of October for Paris Fashion Week, which she was due to attend. She was seen on the front row in a stylish baby-blue dress at the Ellie Saab show but was without her man after Conor's father voiced his concern that the youngster was neglecting his work.

The *National Enquirer* reported: 'They're totally infatuated, and Robert went nuts when he heard Taylor will send her private plane to pick Conor up and bring him to wherever she is over the next six weeks.'

RFK told his son in no uncertain terms that he needed to focus on his schoolwork.

'Taylor's unhappy, but doesn't want to trigger a rift in the Kennedy family – because she's raring to join it herself someday!' said the source.

However, Ethel was a huge fan of Taylor and, speaking to the *Cape Cod Times* at the annual RFK Golf Tournament, she said: 'I am happy that we'll all be neighbours. I'm thrilled.'

When asked if Taylor was invited to the competition, she said: 'That's the only thing she doesn't do. But we'll have to teach her for next year. You know what she really is? She's game. She had never sailed before – she sailed. She played anything that anyone else was doing.'

Other members of the family had also clearly given Conor their blessing. Speaking of the romance, his uncle, Patrick Kennedy, told website TMZ: 'We love Taylor Swift.

She's been a great friend and we're happy for Conor. If she wants to be in the family, she's already part of it.'

Taylor seemed to have found the man of her dreams. Would her fairy-tale ending come true?

CHAPTER ELEVEN

'To me, intense emotion is red'

Taylor's new album *Red* was two years in the writing, producing and recording and finally hit the shelves on 22 October 2012. Like every enduring pop star, Taylor knew that she would have to reinvent herself and *Red* was the perfect transitional album, hinting at a more mature sound and positioned towards a slightly older fan base than the teenybopper one she started out with.

She was nervous about the album's reception, telling website Digital Spy: 'I get nervous for everything – literally everything. I'm so proud of this record and I think I know my fans well enough to know they're going to like it too. There's a lot of pressure putting an album out all over the world and hoping people everywhere like it. There's a lot of nervousness that goes on in my everyday life that I try to balance out by saying, "It's okay, calm down, everything's going to be alright."'

She had been previewing singles from the album on TV show *Good Morning America* every Monday morning for four weeks, teasing her fans with 30-second clips. Despite that push, Taylor told *Rolling Stone* that she wanted the album to remain a mystery.

'I really want there to be so many surprises left on the record for when it comes out eventually, some collaborations that haven't been talked about and some songs that are definitely what make the album so unique.'

She said she had learned a lot about love, telling Taste of Country: 'I think new things I've learned about myself since *Speak Now* are that love has no rules, you know? It's really just about treating people the right way or the wrong way. It you treat people the right way it's gonna go this way, and if you treat people the wrong way it's gonna go this way. And I think that those are the only rules, and other than that it's this crazy unpredictable thing. You can never ever figure out where you're going to end up, who you're going to end up with, who's going to end up being a good guy, who's going to end up being a bad guy, it's just this free-for-all of just chaotic feelings.'

Taylor's exclusive previews started with a wistful number, 'Begin Again', which marked a stark departure from her slick 'We Are Never Ever Getting Back Together'. The folk pop track was about Taylor falling in love again after a failed relationship. She counted down her ex's failings and the soft and soulful narrative style was slightly more complex than her previous works.

She followed 'Begin Again' with the title track, 'Red',

which was typical Taylor country pop, blending strings and guitar. Talking about the story behind the song, Taylor said: 'I wrote this song about the fact that some things are just hard to forget, because the emotions involved with them were so intense, and to me, intense emotion is red.'

She later told *Billboard* that this track signified a departure for her from her old ground, explaining: 'I think the reason I said that was because I made the record exactly the same way I made the last three. I knew I hadn't jumped out of my comfort zone, which at the time was writing alone and working with Nathan. ['Red'] the song was a real turning point for *Red* the album. When I wrote that song my mind started wandering to all the places we could go. If I were to think outside the box enough, go in with different people, I could learn from and have what they do rub off on me as well as have what I do rub off on them.'

In her album notes, the word SAG was spelled out, which commentators pointed out could stand for Sagittarius, which is Jake Gyllenhaal's star sign, or Screen Actors Guild, which might also suggest the actor was the man she was writing about.

Fans in the UK were lucky enough to hear the first-ever live performance of 'Red' in October, at BBC Radio 1's Teen Awards, where Taylor played on a scarlet-coloured guitar and sang into a bejewelled microphone, while red lights flashed in the background. Dressed in a black lacy top and metallic shorts, she had her lucky number 13 scrawled on her hand, and fans held up posters with the number on, while singing the lyrics back to her. While she was in the country, Taylor also sang a snappy version of 'We Are Never Ever Getting Back Together' on *The X Factor*, in a colourful production where she showed off her incredible legs in a pair of tiny hot pants.

Preview track three was 'I Knew You Were Trouble', co-written with Max Martin and Shellback, who were behind 'We Are Never Ever Getting Back Together'. The track had a dubstep vibe and was the boldest on the album.

She said: 'The song we're releasing tonight . . . it's a song that's one of my favourite songs on the album because it sounds just as chaotic as the feeling was when I wrote it. It's a song about kind of being frustrated with yourself because you have your heart broken and you knew when you first saw that person you saw all these red flags and you just went for it anyway,' she explained. 'So, shame on me.'

The fourth and final promo track, 'State of Grace', used more of an alternative-rock sound, with the critics likening the pounding drumbeats and brash guitar riffs to U2.

Taylor explained: 'I wrote this song about when you first fall in love with someone – the possibilities, kind of thinking about the different ways that it could go. It's a really big sound. To me, this sounds like the feeling of falling in love in an epic way.' In the notes were the words, 'I love you doesn't count after goodbye' and it is presumed that this song is also about the guy who inspired the title track.

The previews culminated in an exclusive appearance on *Good Morning America* on release day, when Taylor wowed the fans outside and studio team with a stunning red dress and her signature lippy and gave an interview to the show's anchor, George Stephanopoulos.

She said: 'I think for me [on] this album I tended to really explore the edges of what I'm allowed to do. Exploring, sort of pushing myself and taking myself out of my comfort zone, which is writing alone, and going and working with my heroes – songwriters which have influenced me my whole career. It really challenged me in the best way possible.'

The following day, she took to the middle of Times Square and belted out 'We Are Never Ever Getting Back Together', 'Red' and vintage hit 'Love Story' to the packed crowd of thousands who had queued for hours to see her. Taylor opted for a black skirt paired with a sparkly black long-sleeved top for her stage outfit, while she wore her hair down and wavy, alongside her hallmark red pout.

Fans raced out to buy the album, which also featured two duets. The first, 'The Last Time', was co-written by and featured Snow Patrol's Gary Lightbody and was rumoured to be about Jake.

Talking to National Public Radio, Taylor said: 'The idea was based on this experience I had with someone who was kind of this unreliable guy. You never know when he's going to leave, you never know when he's going to come back, but he always does come back … It's a really fragile emotion you're dealing with when you want to love someone, but you don't know if it's smart to.'

She also worked with British singer-songwriter Ed Sheeran on 'Everything Has Changed' after she heard his work and really loved it.

Taylor said to Digital Spy: 'The first time I heard Ed's music was when I was in Australia and I saw his video for "Lego House" with Rupert Grint in it. I fell in love with his music and I couldn't believe we hadn't had his album come out in the US yet. So I reached out to his management to see if he wanted to write, but at the same time he was reaching out to my management as well. So it was very strange, but I let his management know that anywhere he was on tour I'd fly there and write with him. He came to LA and we ended up writing our duet, "Everything Has Changed".'

However, rather than write in the comfort of the studio, the pair got busy penning the track while sitting on a trampoline in Taylor's garden.

'We, for real, [were] sitting on my trampoline in my back yard 'cause we had been writing a song and I was like, "Hey, I just got a trampoline. You want to see it?" And so, he brought the guitar for some reason,' Taylor recalled to MTV News. 'We ended up writing an entire song out there. For portions of the song, [we were bouncing around] 'cause it's a trampoline and it's fun, and the combined maturity level of both of us is eight years old.'

And although the two musicians come from different musical backgrounds, Ed revealed that their partnership worked.

'Well, I don't really write so much with other artists,' he said. 'Like the Taylor session, when we got together and wrote was the second time I've ever gotten with another singer-songwriter and written a song with them. So it wasn't actually too hard of an adjustment. We're very much alike musically and it worked out well, I think.'

Taylor loved Ed's music, explaining: 'He comes from such a sincere place as a writer, and his songs move you in every direction emotionally. That's something I was so inspired by.'

She also admitted that she doesn't listen to much music while she writes new songs but Ed was on her tracklist.

'Just because I want to be inspired solely on the emotion, just based on how it feels. And so the only artists that I really listened to were Snow Patrol and Ed Sheeran, and that's the reason I wanted to collaborate with those people on the record.'

Other highlights included upbeat '22', a feel-good song about being young and living for the moment. The notes read, 'Ashley, Dianna, Claire and Selena', so the song was obviously written for her friends Ashley Avignone, Dianna Agron, Claire Kislinger and Selena Gomez.

Her romance with Conor and friendship with the Kennedys also featured. 'Everything Has Changed', which Taylor wrote with Ed Sheeran, is about falling in love, and the message in the notes reads, 'Hyannis Port', while the rousing 'Starlight' said, 'For Ethel' and was about Ethel's romance with Robert F. Kennedy.

Taylor told *Us Weekly*: 'I saw a picture of Ethel and Bobby from when they were seventeen at a dance and I just started humming the melody. Sometimes other people's stories inspire me, not always just mine.'

The album was an immediate hit and sold a staggering

1,208,000 copies in its first week, debuting straight at the top of the *Billboard* 200 chart. It was the second fastest-selling album in over a decade, only just behind Britney Spears's *Oops! . . . I Did It Again*.

On hearing the news, she tweeted: 'They just told me *Red* sold 1.2 million albums first week. How is this real life?! You are UNREAL. I love you so much. Thanks a million ;)'

By three weeks in, it had almost sold a staggering 2 million copies.

'This is a crazy feeling,' she said at a listening party at the store Target. 'I mean, these are songs that I've worked on for two years and worked so hard to make different from everything I've done before, and the fans are really getting that. I love that they are understanding that this is something completely new, and it's just a wonderful feeling.'

She was delighted that the fans loved her fresh sound and was interested to hear what their favourite tracks were.

'They are all telling me their favourites,' she said. 'It's so much fun, because their favourites determine my set list for my shows on tour next year. It determines a lot, so I'm just loving seeing the iTunes [songs] chart and getting to see which ones are floating to the top, and I will sit there and go, "I didn't expect that. That's a really personal, emotional song. I didn't expect that to be right there at the top of the iTunes chart."'

Red eventually spent sixteen non-consecutive weeks at No. 1 on *Billboard*'s Country Albums chart. It became Taylor's first chart-topper in the UK, and also peaked at the top of the album charts in twelve countries, including Australia, Canada, Ireland and New Zealand. The album sold 1.89 million copies in its first three weeks and became the second biggest-selling album of the year in the USA. Taylor was bowled over.

It wasn't just the fans who lapped it up; the critics also loved it. The *Guardian* proclaimed: '*Red* is another chapter in one of the finest fantasies pop music has ever constructed,' while *Rolling Stone* declared: 'Her self-discovery project is one of the best stories in pop. When she's really on, her songs are like tattoos' and found influences of Joni Mitchell and U2.

Billboard added: 'As she settles into her superstar persona at the age of twenty-two, Swift has made it clear that she is never going to be pigeonholed, and will always strive for relatable transcendence. *Red* is her most interesting full-length to date, but it probably won't be when all is said and done in her career.'

AllMusic website declared: 'Although she can still seem a little gangly in her lyrical details – her relationship songs are too on the nose and she has an odd obsession about her perceived persecution by the cool kids – these details hardly undermine the pristine pop confections surrounding them. If anything, these ungainly, awkward phrasings humanize this mammoth pop monolith: she's constructed something so precise its success seems preordained, but underneath it all, Taylor is still twitchy, which makes *Red* not just catchy but compelling.'

4Music online summed up with: 'Prepare for a large serving

of soul and tenderness alongside a huge dollop of talent. It's not all country, it's not all pop and that's what makes this album so appealing. You just cannot pin Taylor down to a specific genre, making the album one incredibly varied and enjoyable listen.'

Taylor then started a relentless promotional campaign. Representatives from 72 worldwide radio stations were flown to Nashville during release week for individual interviews with Taylor and she also did a number of TV interviews including David Letterman's *Late Show*, *The View*, *The Ellen DeGeneres Show*, *Dancing with the Stars* and Katie Couric.

It was during her interview with Katie Couric that she hinted all might not be well with Conor.

Taylor said: 'I don't know how to have a normal relationship because I try to act normal and love from a normal place and live a normal life, but there is sort of an abnormal magnifying glass, like a telescope lens, on everything that happens.' She went on: 'I don't know how to do that correctly or anything . . . I don't really know that much about love, it turns out.'

She also talked to *Harper's Bazaar* about what she is looking for in a relationship – a man who is equal to her.

She explained: 'It needs to be equal. If I feel too much like I'm wearing the pants, I start to feel uncomfortable and then we break up. Relationships are the ultimate collaboration but it's wonderful to hand over the reins to your boyfriend when you control so much of these big, high-pressure decisions, you know? That is a huge defining factor in who you choose to be with.'

While clearly her romance with Conor had informed a number of romantic songs on her album, the relationship had gone sour. It was soon reported that it was over, with friends saying Taylor was getting serious too quickly for the young heir to handle.

'Conor's just an 18-year-old kid and wasn't ready for anything superserious,' a pal told Radar Online. 'But Taylor is looking for her soulmate and it kind of freaked him out with how strong she came on.'

The friend also said that Taylor was obsessed with the Kennedy family and was living out a fairy-tale with Conor.

They continued: 'She was more obsessed with the idea of dating a Kennedy, than the actual Kennedy she was dating.'

Other sources said the split was more amicable and a result of their busy lives and the fact they struggled to see one another.

One told *Us Weekly*: 'They quietly parted ways a while ago. It was just a distance thing. No hard feelings. They're fine.'

The source added: 'It's been over a month since they've even seen each other. With her promotion for *Red*, she has no time off until the end of the year.'

Taylor wouldn't need any distraction from the break-up because, after her week of intense promotions, she announced that she would go on tour – and she said she couldn't wait to get back on the road.

Taylor had clearly been thinking about her next tour for some time, telling *Rolling Stone*: 'When I write a song, the first thing I think about is, "Okay, this is a message to

a person, what are they gonna think when they hear it?" . . .
The second thing I think of is, "Ooh, how are we gonna
play this in concert? What's the lighting gonna be like?
What costumes are we gonna have?" So the visual part of
the story comes to me pretty quickly after I write the
song.'

During a radio interview, she said: 'It's nothing like any
other tour before.' However, she added to *Billboard* that it
would be a mix of old and new.

'I'm going to be playing "Love Story" for the rest of my
career because the fans really like it. If I ever get sick of it, I
would continue to play it at my shows. You have to, as an
artist, remember your experiences as a fan. And as a fan you
heard the song in your bedroom, you played it over and over
again, you know where the fiddle part is, you know where
the banjo part is and you like the way it is sung on the
record. I don't see me altering the way my previous work
sounds live because people want to hear it the way they
heard it on record. I don't need to do a jazz version of "Tim
McGraw".

'That being said, we've done some fun mash-ups. Sometimes it's fun to weave someone else's song into your song
as a surprise. I'm always balancing – how much new material do people want to hear, how much old material – and at
the end of the day I'm trying to put on a show that accu-
rately represents where I am now.'

She said in a video announcement on her website: 'As
you may know, my new album *Red* is finally out and I
am so happy about that and I am beyond excited to tell

you that I am coming back out on tour next year and I can't wait to play these songs for my fans. We are starting with 58 shows in 45 cities in 29 states and three provinces. Nine stadiums and 36 arenas. We're starting on March 13, that's my lucky number, in Omaha, Nebraska, through until September.'

When the tickets for the much-anticipated tour eventually went on sale, they were snapped up within minutes by her hoards of fans. The two shows in LA sold out in under a minute and four extra shows were added to try to match the demand.

Taylor also revealed her support act would be her close friend Ed Sheeran. She said: 'I'm bringing someone pretty amazing with me on tour to open up the shows: Ed Sheeran.'

With her relationship with Conor over and Ed sporting a new tattoo with the logo of Taylor's album on his arm, rumours started to gather pace that she and Ed were more than just writing partners. However, Taylor insisted she was single and talked about finding love again in an interview with *Cosmopolitan* magazine:

'I need that unexplainable spark. I just need to see someone and feel, "Oh, no, uh-oh",' she smiled. 'It's only happened a few times in my life, but I feel like if I was gonna be with someone forever, it would be because I saw them and I thought, "Oh, no."'

As for the future, Taylor declared the only thing that could take her away from music is starting a family.

'Being a mom full time, doing everything for my kids, having a bunch of them,' she admitted. 'One day, I'm sure.

But that's the only other thing that could be as thrilling for me as doing this.'

The 46th annual CMA Awards took place on 1 November. Taylor made a dazzling entrance in a floor-length, intricately detailed red Jenny Packham gown, with her hair in loose waves. Co-hosts Carrie Underwood and Brad Paisley took the opportunity to tease her about the recent split. During their opening monologue, they mentioned the couple before Carrie whispered in Brad's ear, apparently informing him of their break-up.

'What? Why don't I ever hear about these things?' he responded, feigning shock. 'I'm the last one to know.'

He then teased: 'Are they ever gonna get back together?' – referring to her track 'We Are Never Ever Getting Back Together'.

Carrie duly replied: 'Never, never, never . . . Never ever.'

However, the camera didn't pan over Taylor to see her reaction.

Later in the evening, Taylor changed into a short red dress to sing 'Begin Again', for which the audience gave her a standing ovation. Taylor was nominated in the categories of Entertainer of the Year, Female Vocalist of the Year and Musical Event of the Year for 'Safe & Sound' with The Civil Wars, but she left the awards show empty-handed.

A few days later, she went on a whistlestop tour of Europe. In London, she turned on the Westfield Christmas lights dressed in a calf-length, 1950s-style dress.

'Whether it's a summertime dress that makes me feel carefree, an evening cocktail dress that makes me feel fancy or a vintage dress that makes me feel like a '50s housewife – which I enjoy feeling like, for some reason – I just really like dresses,' she told *Harper's Bazaar*. 'I'm in a predicament where I can't wear a dress twice or else it's pointed out in magazines, so unfortunately, I have to shop for dresses all the time.'

She performed three songs for a crowd of 10,000 that had turned up to see her. They shouted her name and waved banners and number 13s at her.

'This is unbelievable. This is incredible. It's unreal,' she said. 'I can't seem to stay away from the UK, can I? . . . I like to say "Hi" to the fans because they're so cute and I love the accents.'

She was joined on stage by a group of young ambassadors from Save the Children and advised potential singers to persist in pursuing their dreams.

'It's important to love it until it becomes all-consuming to your life,' she said. 'Sometimes you can get too ahead of yourself and you give up if it doesn't happen for you quickly. Singing should be all you want to do even if you end up singing in a coffee house. That's what I would be doing now if I hadn't had an incredible streak of luck.'

She also flew into Paris and then on to Frankfurt in Germany, where she attended the MTV European Music Awards (EMA). She was up for five gongs.

'I've always wanted to go to the EMA, because you hear about the spectacle of it, and how everyone just goes all out for their performances,' she said to MTV. 'To be nominated for five EMAs was the most exciting feeling, and I was absolutely blown away. I can't wait to be there this year and perform on the show!'

In the end, Taylor, who sported a J. Mendel dress on the red carpet, was a big winner on the night. Wiping the floor with the competition, the singer made off with gongs for Best Female, Best Live and Best Look. Kanye West, who was also there, also managed to stay glued to his seat through-out.

And despite suffering from a sore throat, she wowed the audience with her energetic circus-inspired performance of 'We Are Never Ever Getting Back Together', dressed as a ringmaster.

Taking to Twitter after the ceremony, Taylor wrote: 'Such an insane night!!! You guys won me 3 EMAs! Best female, best live act, best look. Can't even begin to thank you enough. I love you!!'

In November, she also had a busy night at the American Music Awards, where she picked up the gong for Favorite Female Country Artist, thanking her fans with the words: 'I'm stoked . . . I'm really, really happy right now and that's all because of you.'

Moments later, she was back on stage for an electrifying performance of her dubstep hit 'I Knew You Were Trouble', even managing to change outfits mid-song, ripping off her white dress to reveal a sexy red corset and fishnet tights in a masquerade-ball theme. It was her third outfit of the night: on the red carpet she wore a gorgeous short, lacy, beaded

Zuhair Murad gown, which showed off her figure to per-fection.

It was a small taste of what fans might see in her forth-coming Red tour.

'I like for it to be big – as big as possible,' Taylor promised to *Billboard*. 'If we can make a show that dazzles people more than the last tour then I'll have done my job in the right way.'

She added: 'I think one of my favourite things about the Red tour is that one of the main focuses I had was incorpo-rating the element of surprise, and incorporating the unexpected. I really like to think that a good concert can be like a good book; it can take you away, it can take you to a different place and help you escape, and I think that's the main goal for me – helping the fans to escape, if only just for one night.'

Red also spawned a number of singles: 'Begin Again' dropped on 1 October and shot to No. 1 on iTunes and debuted at No. 7 on the *Billboard* 200. 'I Knew You Were Trouble' was released on 14 November and debuted at No. 3.

Life seemed brilliant for the star, but even she conceded that she didn't know what was around the corner.

'I've kind of realised that I have no idea where I'm going to be next year, or in six months, or in two months,' she said to *Wonderland* magazine. 'I mean, I know where I'll be on tour in two months, but have no idea where I'm going to be mentally, emotionally, dreams, goals, wishes, hopes. I have no idea if I'm going to get married or be single forever or have a family or just be on my own. You know, paint in a cottage by the ocean by myself. I just have no idea and I'm kind of into that.

'You can make a board for all the goals you want in your life with the pictures on it, and that's great, daydreaming is wonderful, but you can never plan your future.'

CHAPTER TWELVE

'I think every girl's dream is to find a bad boy at the right time, when he wants to not be bad anymore'

She had dated a member of 'America's Royal Family', a Hollywood A-lister and a best-selling singer, but Taylor's love life was suddenly going to get a lot more interesting.

Harry Styles is the 'flirty' one of British group One Direction (or 1D, as they are also known) who rose to fame on the British version of *The X Factor*, back in 2010. Despite only coming third in the competition, the boys – Harry, Zayn Malik, Niall Horan, Liam Payne and Louis Tomlinson, who were put together by the show's judges – had enjoyed almost overnight superstardom after signing a £2 million record deal with Simon Cowell's label Syco.

Like Taylor, they embraced social media and became international heartthrobs, selling 14 million singles and 8 million albums along the way, with millions of teenage girls watching their every move. They also became record holders when both their first and second albums, *Up All Night* and *Take Me Home*, debuted at the top of the *Billboard* Top 200. Their second offering became the year's third highest debut, just behind Taylor's *Red* and Mumford & Son's *Babel*. Their success Stateside was unexpected and unparalleled, even by the Beatles in the 1960s.

Baby-faced Harry, who hails from the picture-postcard town of Holmes Chapel in Cheshire, had a reputation as a ladies' man and as someone who was reported to like older women after dating *Xtra Factor* host Caroline Flack and having a fling with a married radio DJ, Lucy Horobin, who were both a decade his senior.

He was eighteen when Taylor first met him in March 2012 at the Nickelodeon Kids' Choice Awards. After Harry and Taylor met, he coyly described her as 'nice' and she was seen dancing along to 1D's performance at the Nickelodeon Awards.

At the awards ceremony, apparently, she told Justin Bieber how much she fancied Harry, while Justin joked about keeping his girlfriend Selena away from the band. Apparently, Taylor went backstage and said 'Hi' to the guys in their dressing room, and made everyone laugh by dramatically fanning herself afterwards.

Justin said: 'I already know one of the biggest artists in the world thinks Harry is so hot but I have been sworn to secrecy.'

Harry had always voiced the fact that he found Taylor attractive and, after they met, he told *Seventeen* magazine: 'She honestly couldn't be a sweeter person. She's genuinely nice and extremely talented, and she deserves everything she has.'

Subsequently, it emerged that the couple may have had a fling after this – while Harry was in the States – and that she was heartbroken when she later saw pictures of Harry kissing Emma Ostilly while 1D were on tour in New Zealand, but then hooked up with Conor.

A source told Radar Online: 'Taylor really liked Harry and even though they weren't exclusive, he hinted at making it official with her just before he took off to Australia. He even told Taylor he didn't want her to see anybody else while he was gone.'

Many people then concluded that her track 'I Knew You Were Trouble' was written about Harry.

A source told Radar Online: 'Taylor was crushed over Harry the first time they dated, and like she always does, she penned a song about him to deal with her broken heart. "I Knew You Were Trouble" is one hundred per cent about Harry. She knew he was young and popular with the ladies and wasn't ready for a serious relationship, but somehow hoped she could make it work.'

According to the insider, Taylor penned the track during one of the pair's break-ups.

'She was head over heels for Harry so even though she knew he was bad news for her, she gave him another chance,' the source said.

After rumours surfaced that they had been texting one another, Harry was asked about it on an Australian radio show, where he said at the time: 'We met in America, and she's very nice . . .' Later, it was noted that they wore the same necklace just days after each other.

Early in November, they were seen holding hands backstage on the US *X Factor*, where they were both due to perform. During rehearsals, Harry even joined Taylor's mum Andrea in the audience to watch her soundcheck before running on stage, tackling her and throwing her over his shoulder and dashing off again.

Taylor blew the crowd away with her live TV debut performance of 'State of Grace', wearing a simple sheer long-sleeved top, paired with black trousers, vintage leather shoes and a fedora hat.

Radio-show host Mario Lopez confirmed he saw the pair 'walking hand in hand', telling listeners: 'Taylor Swift was the special guest performer, and [here's] a little inside scoop for you. During rehearsals, Harry from One Direction came and slapped me on the back, and said, "Hey, Mario, how ya doing?" And I said, "What are you doing here?" And he sort of [pointed] toward Taylor.'

Mario said he later saw them 'walking off hand in hand. So Taylor Swift and Harry from One Direction – you heard it here first. [They're] officially hanging out, I can say that much.'

And the official US *X Factor* Twitter page sent Twittersphere into meltdown with the words: 'Together in the lunch line (Cheeseburgers) laughing & smiling was @Harry_Styles & @taylorswift13! :) #internationalpoproyalty.'

The pair were quickly dubbed 'Haylor' and officially knocked Justin and Selena off the pedestal of coolest celeb couple.

More speculation ensued, with *Look* magazine claiming that Taylor had instructed an estate agent to find her a home near Harry's pad in North London.

A source told the magazine: 'She's been interested in buying a house in the UK for a while. But after months of not really mentioning it, Taylor's suddenly instructed an estate agent to get on it ASAP! She's even asked Harry if he'll come and look at some places with her, since he knows the area.'

It has never been confirmed if Taylor bought a property in the UK, but she has openly admitted that she was looking for a 'bad boy' to tame.

'There's a really interesting charisma involved . . .' she told *Parade* magazine. 'They usually have a lot to say, and even if they don't, they know how to look at you to say it all. I think every girl's dream is to find a bad boy at the right time, when he wants to not be bad anymore.'

She also revealed that she struggled to pace herself when it came to falling in love.

'I don't think there's an option for me to fall in love slowly, or at medium speed. I either do or I don't. I don't think it through, really, which is a good thing and a bad thing. You don't look before you leap, which is like, "Yay, this is awesome! Let's not think twice!" And then you're like, "We used to be flying. Now we're falling. What's happening?"'

Clearly, she was smitten with the curly-haired heartthrob

but work was always her priority and, at the end of November, she cut a lonely figure as she flew solo to Japan to promote *Red*. Spotted at Narita International Airport, she carried her guitar in a case and stopped for fans and posed for pictures.

She had clearly been practising her Japanese and, at the end of October, on David Letterman's *Late Show*, she showed off a few choice phrases. She knew she would be spending the Thanksgiving holiday in Japan and joked: 'It's gonna be interesting trying to find turkey . . .'

She performed on a few TV and radio shows before heading to Australia, where she attended the ARIA Awards – the Australian version of the Grammys – in Sydney. Dressed in an immaculate Ellie Saab Grecian-inspired cream dress, featuring cutaway details at the side and a chic hairstyle, she looked in her element as she signed autographs for fans and stopped for photographers.

She wrote on her Twitter page: 'Woah. The fans at the ARIAs came out in full force!! This is INSANE!'

Prior to the event, she also penned: 'So excited about performing on the ARIAs tonight! Never been before. Here comes 'trouble' . . . See what I did there? Sorry. I know. Sorry.'

Once inside the Sydney Entertainment Centre, she ditched her dress and changed into a cute red-and-white baseball jacket, high-waisted navy shorts and a striped top, to perform 'Here Comes Trouble'. During the energetic rendition, she even threw one male dancer into the air.

And Taylor certainly seemed to be enjoying her new

surroundings, posting a snap of herself posing with a mini-Australian flag on her Twitter page.

Alongside the picture, she wrote: 'In the dressing room at the ARIAs. Loving Australia.'

Australia was clearly loving Taylor too and, as she arrived at the airport to go home, many fans gathered to wish her goodbye, took pictures and asked for her autograph.

On her return to Los Angeles, Taylor's first engagement, on 1 December, was the KIIS FM Jingle Ball, where she was one of the superstar headlining acts. The singer, who rocked a monochrome striped dress on the red carpet, closed the show by performing her hits 'State of Grace', 'You Belong with me', 'Love Story', 'I Knew You Were Trouble', and 'We Are Never Ever Getting Back Together', using her signature red mic. It was the first time she had performed at an event where her ex, Joe Jonas, was also singing, since they split in 2008.

The *Los Angeles Times* wrote about how her performances – and good-natured outlook – had changed: 'It's been noted that with her venom-seeping, megawatt-produced album *Red*, she's pretty much become the Evil Taylor from her video for "You Belong With Me". What's unexpected is how good a look all this is for her – the first artist to start in banjo-flecked country and grow to make sense of brooding dubstep ("I Knew You Were Trouble") and bemused cheerleader pop ("We Are Never Ever Getting Back Together"), whose titanic Max Martin chorus is worth every penny they paid for it . . . At Jingle Ball, she wore it as a skeptical sneer, one likely aimed at her myriad exes (woe to be Conor Kennedy on the receiving end of her next album) and her own stereotypes. Hopefully, Jingle Ball's undercard took notes – that's how you grow up onstage.'

The following day, Taylor and Harry were first snapped publicly together enjoying a romantic stroll through New York's iconic Central Park Zoo, hugging a friend's baby and looking totally loved-up. Taylor was dressed down in a burgundy jacket and Harry was wearing his trademark beanie, a shirt and khaki jacket.

The next day, she was seen out on her own on the New York streets dressed in skinny jeans and a blue jumper. She had a big night ahead: first up was the Ripple of Hope Gala at New York's Marriott Marquis, where she was honoured with an award by the Kennedy family for her philanthropic efforts, which is given to individuals who 'reflect Robert Kennedy's passion for equality, justice, basic human rights . . .'. Past honorees have included President Bill Clinton, Archbishop Desmond Tutu, Bono, George Clooney and Vice President Al Gore.

As Taylor went up to collect her award, dressed in a mid-length Oscar de la Renta dress and peep-toe shoes, the Kennedy family couldn't say enough good things about her.

Kerry Kennedy gushed: 'Taylor Swift is just the kind of woman we want our daughters to be.' Adding, 'This world demands the qualities of youth: not a time of life but a state of mind, a temper of the will, a quality of imagination, a predominance of courage over timidity, of the appetite for adventure over the life of ease. Here's a young woman – twenty-two years old – who has put herself out in the world, and in an incredibly powerful and strong way.'

In addition to picking up her award, Taylor sang 'Starlight', her song about Ethel Kennedy, in front of a celeb-packed crowd, which included her good friend Dianna Agron as well as Antonio Banderas, Melanie Griffith and Mia Farrow. Afterwards, she posed with members of the Kennedy family but, interestingly Taylor's ex, Conor, was nowhere to be seen.

Later in the evening, she traded her gold dress for a little black dress and black ballet pumps and sprinted across to Madison Square Garden, where One Direction had been playing a sold-out gig to a crowd of 20,000 screaming fans. Joining the boys, their girlfriends and families, she hopped on the large tour bus to the after-party at New York's Hudson hotel. She looked every inch the perfect pop-star girlfriend.

The girls, friends and family went through the main entrance of the swanky celebrator bash, while the boys and Taylor sneaked through the back door to avoid drawing attention to themselves. Harry then introduced his new superstar love to his mum, Anne, and the smitten duo were said to have recreated the *Dirty Dancing* lift to the song, '(I've Had) The Time of My Life' on the dance floor, while other guests laughed and egged them on. Harry was also seen singing a very bad version of Elton John and Kiki Dee's 'Don't Go Breaking My Heart' on the karaoke machine with Ed Sheeran, while Taylor looked on.

After the lavish party, they were spotted holding hands returning to the same hotel at 4 a.m., and the following day they emerged though the lobby doors just moments apart.

Then that night, Harry was seen arriving at Taylor's hotel with his head down and an overnight bag slung over his shoulder at 11 p.m., just an hour after she had finished doing some recording at New York's City Pier 59 Studios.

The following morning, he emerged in a fresh white 'LONDON LOVES LA' T-shirt and a slightly messy hairdo, surrounded by his minders. The couple had clearly been making the most of their time together and outwitting the paparazzi wasn't an option.

From there, Taylor headed back to Nashville to host the Grammy Nominations Concert, alongside rapper LL Cool J. She even gamely beat-boxed on a gangster hit 'Mean' and said: 'I'm a hundred per cent sure we're not going to be nominated for that collaboration next year.' Much to her delight, she also learned that she was up for Record of the Year for her hit song 'We Are Never Ever Getting Back Together' and Best Country Duo/Group Performance and Best Song Written for Visual Media for 'Safe & Sound'.

Clearly, Haylor had fallen hard for each other and wanted to spend as much time together as possible, so Taylor hot-footed it back to New York where she was seen with Harry again, leaving her hotel on their way to a romantic dinner date. Harry was dressed in a black fur-collared jacket, brown T-shirt and jeans, while his girlfriend wore a brown jacket over a dress and stripy tights.

From there, they went to the Crosby Street Hotel, where they were met by some of Taylor's friends, including actresses Emma Stone and Dianna Agron. As the world buzzed with the news of the new couple, Ed Sheeran confirmed the question on everyone's lips when he was asked, nodding before saying: 'I mean, the papers are saying it.'

Tellingly, Taylor opened up to the British version of *Cosmopolitan*, talking about her troubled love life in the past and her hopes for the future.

When asked what she doesn't know about relationships, she said: 'How to make them last. I've never had a really long relationship, so I have no idea what that's like . . . Wish me luck for the future!'

She added: 'I really don't have any rules about dating when it comes to height, age, career choice, anything like that. It doesn't matter. It's really more about strength of character. When it comes to age I've been all over the map!'

1D had one final appearance in the USA at Z100's Jingle Ball at Madison Square Garden in New York on 7 December. On the red carpet, Harry joked about with a sprig of mistletoe, kissing girls who walked past. When he was asked what he thought about the amount of attention the relationship was getting, he coyly responded: 'I just bumped into her at the zoo and then I don't know . . .' Backstage, there are pictures of Taylor giving Harry a kiss on the cheek before he bounded on stage with the rest of 1D.

From there, Harry was heading home to the UK for the Capital FM Jingle Bell Ball and Taylor offered him a flight on her private jet. He accepted and they spent a precious few hours together.

Once they touched down, 1D had just a short time to rehearse for the event and Taylor was whisked to the VIP Area to watch the show, which featured performances by

JLS, Little Mix, Rizzle Kicks and Cheryl Cole, who duetted with her manager, Will.i.am. Later, the boys from the band Lawson posted a snap of themselves with her.

Rumours surfaced that while Harry was happy to spend hours canoodling with his new love, the rest of the band were less than impressed with the time they were spending together. Taylor – who was seen with Harry backstage at the *X Factor* final in Manchester on 9 December – was later branded as the band's 'Yoko Ono', drawing comparisons between Taylor and John Lennon's artist wife, who was said to be responsible when the Beatles' split in 1970.

A source said: 'There was loads of room for the rest of the band in Taylor's luxury jet but he didn't even suggest they travelled together. It's not really far off from the Yoko situation.'

Next up was a magical mini-break for the couple, who headed north so Harry could introduce Taylor to his older sister, Gemma. Harry and Gemma are extremely close and he really wanted her to meet his new girlfriend.

While they were away, the pair also got to spend Taylor's twenty-third birthday together. Stepping out for a celebratory lunch, Harry looked thrilled as he took her for a meal at the George & Dragon in Great Budworth, Cheshire. Taylor looked gorgeous in a pea-green coat, skinny jeans and stylish brogues as she held hands with Harry. She was overheard telling Gemma, 'He's amazing.' Later that day, a picture emerged online of the pair at the local Chinese takeaway, taken by a friend who tweeted: 'Just casually finding Taylor Swift in the Chinese.'

On her birthday Harry was said to have bought Taylor gifts worth £1,000, including a £400 Jimmy Choo handbag, antique earrings and a vintage photo frame containing a black-and-white photo of the couple. He apparently also surprised her with twenty-three cupcakes, which he'd personally picked out from a bakery.

The Custom Cupcake Company owner Matt Blakeley said: 'The woman [who ordered the cupcakes] said it was for Harry Styles but I didn't know who that was at first. We had got a lot of orders before Christmas, but she said she desperately needed them so we said okay.'

Taylor's birthday came at the end of their trip, which saw Harry show Taylor around the local area. Dressed up for the cold weather, they enjoyed a day in picturesque Bowness-on-Windermere, where they strolled through the village, stopping at the Pandora jewellery shop and the World of Beatrix Potter, and were pictured feeding doves together with Harry's mum. One of the birds took a peck at Taylor's handbag, also thought to be a present from Harry.

The following day, they went for a walk in the Peak District and had dinner with Gemma at the Rising Sun in Hope Valley, where Taylor apparently tucked into the local delicacy – black pudding – followed by lemon sole, while Harry devoured a turkey roast, followed by Christmas pudding.

Pub manager Sarah Walker explained: 'Taylor said she was loving being in Britain and she also seemed to like being in the countryside. She said she didn't mind the cold. They were both lovely and she's a honey.'

While she was in the UK, Harry was said to have got Taylor hooked on one of his favourite comedy TV programmes, *The Inbetweeners*, which she found really funny.

Thankfully, Taylor was away from her Nashville home when a man was arrested in the grounds in the early hours one morning after he scaled the 6-feet fence. According to website TMZ, Jacob Kulke told security men that he was her boyfriend and he had got the bus from Wisconsin to be with her on her birthday and surprise her. He was taken into custody but the charges were later dropped.

This was the more unnerving side of her life and, along with the paparazzi constantly trying to picture her, Taylor often felt overwhelmed.

'I don't know necessarily how much privacy I'm entitled to, but I know I don't get much of it,' she told *Parade*. 'At the same time, I asked for this. I could be playing in a coffee house. I'd be happy doing that, [but] not as happy, probably. Knowing that people are going to hear the music I make is the most amazing feeling. Knowing that there are dudes waiting outside my house with cameras, hiding in the bushes, is a less awesome feeling.'

Harry later drove Taylor to Manchester Airport, where her private jet was waiting to take her to Germany. There, she completed a number of promotional commitments, including a performance of 'We Are Never Ever Getting Back Together' live on the TV show *Schlag de Raab*.

The pair kept in touch on the phone and Harry's friend Radio 1 DJ Nick 'Grimmy' Grimshaw, confirmed that Harry was smitten with Taylor, telling the *Daily Mirror*: 'Harry really likes Taylor, he's fallen for her in a big way. At first, I wasn't sure if the relationship was a real one but I talk to him a lot and it seems to be that she's the one for him – for now, anyway.'

He also praised her fun attitude, adding: 'American artists are usually really, really boring and reserved but Taylor is fun. She's always up for a laugh and is really good company.

'Harry likes people who make him laugh. I talk to Harry a lot on the phone while he's away touring and he talks about her a lot. He is very happy with her. I like her a lot too; she came on my show recently and we had a really fun time.'

A day later, the couple were reunited in LA, where they were seen at the Shamrock tattoo parlour. Harry had a large ship etched on his upper arm, next to the heart on his bicep. The design is really similar to the one the male model had on his arm in Taylor's video for the single 'I Knew You Were Trouble'. Harry posed for a series of snaps with the parlour owner and Taylor, who had been playing pool with friends while her man got the artwork done.

Taylor also released her single, 'I Knew You Were Trouble', and tried out an edgier look in the video, which showed her waking up in the morning with pink hair, in a desert littered with rubbish from a rave.

She explained: 'Good girl is living her life, going about her, you know, daily life and all of sudden she runs into this force. This guy is just like a force. . . She'll do anything to fit into his world, including change everything about herself.'

The song debuted at No. 3 on the *Billboard* Hot 100 and

No. 1 on Hot Digital Songs, with 416,000 copies sold in its first week. This was Taylor's second-largest first-week singles sales. It became her fourteenth Top 10 hit and her eleventh song to debut inside the Top 10.

Rumours swirled that the song was about Harry after Taylor released the music video for the track. One scene shows the singer accompanying her fictional boyfriend getting a tattoo – a poignant moment, as she went with Harry in real life on more than one occasion while he got inked.

At the final of the US *X Factor*, as he walked up the red carpet, Harry was asked how Taylor was, and he replied: 'She's good,' while his bandmates mocked him, saying: 'Oh yes, so what do you think of the Haylor situation, then? Another interviewer asked if they were a couple and, in a typical laid-back Harry way, he confirmed they were.

Then Taylor took Harry back home to meet her family. Harry, Taylor and her mum, Andrea, were seen going grocery shopping and later in the day they went through the drive-thru of popular fast-food chain In-N-Out Burger.

Showing just how quickly things were moving between them, the couple jetted to a romantic skiing holiday in Utah, where they were seen having lunch with Taylor's brother, Austin, at the Canyons Resort in Park City. Harry stood out from the crowd in his orange beanie, while Taylor kept her head warm with a fashionable grey handband.

Fans kept each other updated on what was happening between the pair on Twitter. One onlooker tweeted: 'Harry was holding hands with tswift. I saw him first in [a] hot tub outside my condo then on the streets downtown.'

While they were there, the couple also met up with Selena Gomez and Justin Bieber, who were staying in the same luxury resort, The Colony.

It was rumoured that Harry and Taylor planned to spend Christmas together in Australia, as Taylor was going there to promote her new album and play some gigs. Taylor told website The Boot: 'It's gonna be non-stop sun. So it will be weird to have a tan around Christmas but I'm really excited about it.' However, according to the *New York Daily News*, Harry declined, as he wanted to spend Christmas at home.

Even though he wasn't with Taylor, reportedly, he sent her a singagram to let her know he was thinking of her, which she found hilarious. They were also said to have had a long Skype session on their computers.

Taylor was reported to have bought Harry some Beatles memorabilia after looking for rare autographed items she knew that he would love from shops in Liverpool. She was apparently looking to spend between £40,000 and £50,000. Harry also went vintage and bought Taylor an antique emerald bracelet he found in a jewellery store in Cheshire.

The couple couldn't bear to be apart for long and they later reunited for the New Year back in the USA, where Taylor was performing alongside Justin Bieber for *Dick Clark's New Year's Rockin' Eve* in Times Square in New York. Taylor ditched her preppy look for tight black leather trousers and a red jacket, and sang 'We Are Never Ever Getting Back Together' and 'I Knew You Were Trouble'.

'There are 13's EVERYWHERE. This is PERFECT,' she tweeted.

After Taylor's performance, the couple shared a passionate kiss. One fan tweeted: 'Just rode on an elevator with Harry Styles and Taylor Swift while they made out. It was beautiful.' The loved-up pair then went to Times Square to see the New Year crystal ball drop and shared another embrace, which was caught on camera by hundreds of bystanders as everyone around them sang 'Auld Lang Syne'.

They then headed back to their hotel, where Harry apparently declared his love for his new girlfriend. He was really falling for her and knew that she understood exactly what he was going through. Taylor was also clearly thrilled at how her year was going, and tweeted: 'Can't even verbalize how stoked I am for 2013!'

However, Taylor's protective father, Scott, reportedly ordered Harry to slow things down during a man-to-man chat, because he didn't want his daughter's heart to be broken.

A 'source' told the *Sun on Sunday*: 'He likes Harry but he wants them to slow down and take things easy. It's clear to everyone they are smitten with one another and are already talking about marriage. He doesn't want them to split up.'

The New Year started with another jaunt in the sun, when Harry and Taylor jetted off to the British Virgin Islands on New Year's Day for a top-secret holiday. They had both been so busy they needed some time away to relax and they hoped that no one would know where they went. It was only revealed that the pair were there when pictures of them posing with some fans at a restaurant in Virgin Gorda, the third largest of the Caribbean islands, emerged on the Internet. In the snaps Taylor was wearing a mint green spaghetti strap dress and Harry was sporting his favourite orange beanie hat.

It seemed blissful, but Taylor was all too aware of how quickly things can change.

Speaking to the *Guardian*, she said: 'I think the one thing I'm really afraid of is . . . that the magic doesn't last. The butterflies and daydreams and love, all these things I hold so dear, are going to leave some day. I haven't had a relationship that's lasted for ever. I only know about them starting and ending. Those are my fears. I spend a lot of time balancing between faith and disbelief.'

Her fears were well founded: a day later pictures emerged of a downcast and upset-looking Taylor alone on a boat at Virgin Gorda's US Customs, with her hands in her lap, while Harry partied in a hot tub on Necker Island with friends and family of the island's billionaire owner, Richard Branson.

Some claimed the couple were on the rocks after Taylor cryptically tweeted some lyrics from 'I Knew You Were Trouble', the song she had reportedly written about Harry the first time they split up.

It later emerged that they had indeed split, after an 'almighty row', and Taylor left the holiday three days early, on 4 January on the first flight she could get back to the USA. One newspaper said the split came after Taylor nagged him about his intentions towards other women and that he found her 'too demanding', while another said that Taylor was prioritising her own career commitments over Harry's duties towards 1D and, in the heat of the moment, said that he was 'lucky to be with her'.

Radar Online reported that Harry was sick and tired of Taylor talking about homemaking and antiques when all he wanted to do was party. The gossip site also claimed that Taylor was nervous about how she was seen by the public, so she wouldn't 'put out'. They said: 'Taylor is so concerned that the public will think she's a wh*re because she dates around, that she doesn't put out, but what she doesn't get is that the guys keep dumping her because she's being a prude.'

The couple's whirlwind fling had lasted just sixty-five days – and her record label confirmed that she would write a song about the break-up, amid claims she wanted Harry back.

Many critics and fans were more cynical about the romance, speculating it was a set-up.

The *Guardian*'s Lost In Showbiz blog wrote: 'It was inevitable Styles and Swift would get together seeing as, between them, they have allegedly dated every single person on the planet. That this relationship happened to bookend Swift releasing an album and One Direction announcing a tour is just one of those coincidences that often accompanies celebrity relationships. OK, some of their dates might have had the suspicious smack of PR exercises, such as an excursion to The World of Beatrix Potter in Bowness-on-Windermere and a very intimate date to Times Square on New Year's Eve, a place no sober person has ever ventured. But only a cynic would suggest that a relationship between a reality-TV boy-band member and a country-and-western singer was anything but true love in our time. And so, we mourn it with due respect.'

And the *National Enquirer* said: 'Little does Taylor know that Harry's handlers went to great lengths to put the two together because she's such a huge star.' Their source added: 'Anytime Taylor starts dating a new guy she gets a flurry of media attention, and her break-ups receive even more.'

Whatever the true story, Harry's fans rejoiced on Twitter, with messages including: 'hahaha we all knew this day would be soon'; 'let's throw a huge party'; and 'praise god, yippee!' Then people started predicting the names of song titles that Taylor might use if she were to write a break-up song about Harry, like she had with other famous exes. The hashtag #HaylorBreakupSongTitles became a No. 1 trending topic worldwide on Twitter within a few hours after the news broke of the split.

Times like this were bound to be difficult for Taylor, who said: 'What I had to learn to do, in order to maintain a general happiness in my life, was to stop reading everything. And then it gets really bad if you go through a break-up and those blogs have these polls asking, "Who should they date next?" And you're just sitting there staring at the laptop bawling. But you can live in a normal world where a break-up is just a break-up if you don't expose yourself to what's being speculated about yourself. That's where I live now.'

There was more heartbreak for the star. After she left the Virgin Islands, Harry partied alone on Necker Island, where he was seen in a hot tub with another blonde, Hermione Way.

The *Sun* said: 'He couldn't keep his eyes off her all the time he was there. Harry was fuming as the row with Taylor got really bitter and a lot of things were said that they both didn't mean. But by the time he arrived at Sir Richard's place and saw the luxury and women holidaying there, he soon calmed down.'

Just to add to that, Hermione tweeted: 'To all the journalists hounding me this morning – I have nothing to say on the Harry story. What happens on Necker, stays on Necker.'

Whatever had happened on Necker, Taylor was devastated. She really thought Harry could have been 'The One'.

CHAPTER THIRTEEN

'There's a special place in hell for women who don't help other women'

Taylor knew what it was like to feel heartbroken, but her split from Harry Styles left her feeling a whole range of different emotions.

'It's very complex; you're never feeling just sad,' she told *Wonderland* magazine. 'Maybe you wake up and you feel sad, and then you get angry, and then you feel like "I'm fine", and then you feel confident, and then you feel a sense of doubt, and then you're insecure, and then there's jealousy, and then you're back to sad – and then you feel fine again.'

She wasn't able to mope for long: she had to pick herself back up and attend the People's Choice Awards, where she was Kanye-d on stage by host Olivia Munn. In hilarious scenes, brunette Olivia refused to hand over Taylor's Favorite

Country Artist award, saying it was awkward that the blonde had won.

Taylor, who was wearing a plunging white gown, took the prank in good spirits and laughed. 'This always happens to me . . . God!' she said.

With her hands firmly on her new trophy, she added: 'I want to thank the fans because this is a fan voted award and I absolutely love you with all of my heart. I want to thank radio and I want to thank the fans for calling radio and being like, "Play her music" – thank you for doing that. You guys have blown my mind with what you've done for this album, *Red*, and I just want to thank you for caring about my music and for caring about me. Thank you so much, you guys, I love you.'

The awkward moments kept piling up for Taylor, as she left the stage to the music of One Direction's hit, 'Live While We're Young'. And afterwards, there were also reports that she was on the rebound and had asked actress Jennifer Lawrence to introduce her to actor Bradley Cooper, who 'politely declined' her advances. According to Radar Online: 'He thinks she's far too young for him and wants someone his own age.'

After the event, she tried to show she was fine and tweeted: 'Sitting here with my new People's Choice award and Chinese food takeout, watching *Law & Order*. Thank you for a beautiful night.'

Taylor soon sought comfort in the recording studio and tweeted a picture of herself with her guitar, sitting cross-legged and scribbling lyrics in her notebook, alongside the words: 'Somewhere in LA.' Perhaps in warning to Harry, she also penned the words: 'Back in the studio . . . Uh oh.'

There were reports that she had written as many as five songs about how she was feeling towards him. A source told The *Sun* newspaper: 'Taylor writes music in the same way that other women chat to their friends on the phone. It's been how she deals with her emotions for most of her life. Harry and Taylor only dated for a short time but there were very strong feelings, so it's been a tough comedown.'

She was said to be worried any new songs she released would be linked to Harry, so she would have to be careful to keep them more cryptic this time. 'Lyrics have been written, but Taylor hasn't come close to deciding whether she'll ever release them', continued the source.

When she was asked by the Daily Beast website if she ever felt guilty for writing about guys, she replied: 'I take these songs and these people who inspire these songs on a case-by-case basis. If there were someone who was a good person, I'm not going to write something bad about them. But if they handle a situation in a way that really messed up my life for a while, that's what I'm going to write about. For me, I've never changed the reason I write a song. Songs for me are like a message in a bottle. You send them out to the world and maybe the person who you feel that way about will hear it someday.'

Her family rallied around her and she was seen having dinner with her parents and brother, Austin, at Mastro's Steakhouse in Beverly Hills. She also leaned on BFF Selena Gomez, who had also recently split with her man, Justin

Bieber, and they planned some girly nights out to try to put their heartache behind them.

'Taylor and Selena are definitely planning some girl nights. Taylor said Harry Styles was a jerk, and said really mean things to her,' a source told Hollywood Life website. 'Selena told her that they were better than those losers, so they can't wait to have a bunch of girls over and dance it out!'

Taylor wanted to show her curly-haired ex what he was missing and looked incredible in a Donna Karan gown at the Golden Globes, where she had a nomination for Best Original Song for 'Safe & Sound'.

Once inside the venue, however, it seems Taylor was the butt of the joke again. She was left mortified by comments by the hosts Tina Fey and Amy Poehler, who said Taylor should stay away from Michael J. Fox's 23-year-old son, Sam, who was acting as the evening's 'Mr Golden Globe', escorting winners to the stage. And that she needed some 'me' time to find out about herself.

The joke went down well with the audience but, as well as upsetting Taylor, the gag didn't sit well with Michael.

'I don't keep up with it at all,' the *Good Wife* star told New York magazine *Vulture* soon after. 'Taylor Swift writes songs about everybody she goes out with, right? What a way to build a career.' The 51-year-old admitted that at first he 'wouldn't even know who she was' if Taylor were to turn up at the family home as Sam's date. But, he added, he would definitely remember her if she were to release a record about his son. Michael said: '"Sam, You Piece of S***." Oh . . . that was the girl you brought home!'

After a huge backlash from Taylor's fans, who went to war with the *Back to the Future* star on Twitter, Taylor confirmed that Michael had got in touch to apologise for his cruel comments.

She posted: 'Hey everybody, Michael J. Fox got in touch with me today and we are good. Thank you for having my back.'

Sam jumped right in and retweeted it, adding, 'hope you gave her my #'

However, apparently, the joke made by the hosts had really upset her.

According to sources at US *Star* magazine: 'She can't snap out of it. Taylor is putting on a brave face to the public but she is a complete mess. Taylor thought Tina's taunt was a low blow and she bawled herself to sleep that night. That's when it hit her that she has such a horrible reputation, it can affect her professionally.'

During an interview in *Vanity Fair* a few weeks later, she fired back at the hosts.

'You know, Katie Couric is one of my favourite people,' she said. 'Because she said to me she had heard a quote that she loved, that said, "There's a special place in hell for women who don't help other women."'

She added in a rare moment of openness about her love life: 'If you want some big revelation, since 2010 I have dated exactly two people. The fact that there are slide shows of a dozen guys that I either hugged on a red carpet or met for lunch or wrote a song with . . . it's just kind of ridiculous.'

She also used an interview in *Elle* to hit back at reports, as she was fed up with being cast as the desperate and needy one.

'I'm sure if I looked up the latest Google Alerts rumour it would say I'm chasing somebody who doesn't like me as much as I like him – people love that angle on me,' she said. 'They're like, "Oh, Taylor, coming on too strong again, chasing boys." I never chase boys. They don't like it!'

Later, Tina Fey, who is best known for her work on *Saturday Night Live*, told *Us Weekly*: 'It was just a joke, and I think it was actually a very benign joke. We, I feel bad that she was upset. I am a feminist, and she is a young and talented girl. That being said, I do agree I am going to hell. But for other reasons. Mostly boring tax stuff.'

Just a day after, comic and talk-show host Chelsea Handler weighed into the row with a theory on why the country star has dated 'so many men'.

Speaking on the *Watch What Happens Live* show, Chelsea joked: 'My theory about Taylor Swift is that she's a virgin, that everyone breaks up with her because they date her for two weeks and she's like, "I'm not gonna do it." And they're like, "Oh, well, forget it. Then I don't want to date you." The guy thinks they're going to de-virginise her, and they're not. She's never going to get de-virginised, ever, ever, ever, ever.'

Clearly, Chelsea was also going to Taylor's special place in hell.

Taylor certainly needed reasons to smile and she finally raised a laugh after veteran Hollywood actor Samuel L. Jackson appeared on Capital FM and gave a unique rendition of 'We Are Never Ever Getting Back Together' that caught her attention. In the clip, Samuel doesn't quite sing over the instrumental; instead, he just talks, while replacing Taylor's original lyrics with some explicit words. The video went viral and, spotting the hilarious soundbite on the Internet, Taylor took to her Twitter account to give her approval, posting a link to the video.

Selena also confirmed that time with Taylor was cheering them both up.

She told *Life & Style Weekly*: 'Taylor is one of the most inspirational, positive, good-hearted people I know. I think she's been a big part of me staying who I am, too. I've been through a lot in the past few months. It's been weird and sad and cool.' She explained: 'We have both experienced the same things at the same time . . . But we've never once talked about our industry. She just became the person I'd go to for an issue with my family or boyfriend. It's so hard to trust girls, so I'm lucky to have her.'

However, Harry was very much still in Taylor's mind. At the end of January, she travelled to the UK and was said to have checked into a hotel near Harry's North London home, amid speculation they were having a secret showdown.

A source told the *Sun*: 'Taylor flew to Luton and then travelled to London yesterday – and there's talk of a meeting with Harry being on the cards. She has no obvious reason or promo duties in London this week. Harry has just got back from a small tour in Japan with the band and now has four days off. Out of all the hotels there are in London, Taylor has opted for one close to Harry's house.'

Afterwards, there would be rumours that the couple wanted to give the romance another go and had planned to stay at the same hotel in Cannes, where they were both performing at the NRJ Music Awards.

'Taylor realised she was being a bit full-on,' an insider told the *Sun*. 'She is now more relaxed about their relationship. She intends to enjoy it more rather than worry about where it could eventually lead. Harry is not the sort of guy you can stay mad at for long. She's given him some space and it's done them both a world of good. What happened over New Year is now a distant memory.'

Taylor was seen smiling and out with her entourage in Madrid, having dinner. 'Quick photo-shoot in London and now we're in Madrid,' she tweeted.

The star continued with her mature style makeover at the 40 Principales Awards, where she showed off her fashion credentials in an incredibly daring white plunging mini-dress. She also made clear just how much her European fans appreciate her when she won the International Artist award and performed 'We Are Never Ever Getting Back Together' and 'Love Story' to rapturous applause.

She was met by a similar response at the NRJ Awards, after performing 'We Are Never Ever Getting Back Together' in a lacy black dress and knee-high leather boots, having changed from a short, plunging Ellie Saab gown.

'If there's a dress that I feel is incredibly fashionable and it's a little more low cut, I'm twenty-three and I feel like it's okay to wear that,' she said to Spanish TV show El Hormiguero. 'You know, if I want to wear shorts on stage, one time when I wore shorts on stage for the first time the press articles were like, "Taylor gets edgy". I'm like, "I'm wearing shorts!"'

Taylor sat through Harry and the rest of 1D's performance before they picked up Best International Group. However, rather than the romantic reunion everyone was waiting for, the couple went out of their way to avoid each other.

'It was very carefully timed so they didn't do the carpet at the same time,' an insider blabbed to *Us Weekly*. 'Taylor didn't do any backstage interviews and didn't use a dressing room – she changed at the hotel because she didn't want to see Harry at any point . . . Things were timed to keep them apart and for it to not become a big media circus.'

There was also no sign of Harry when Taylor boarded a boat party, in a chic all-black outfit, waving to the hundreds of French fans who had crowded on the dock to catch a glimpse of their idol.

The following day, she was seen in Paris with her friend, *True Grit* star Hailee Steinfeld. Using their Twitter and Instagram pages to document the day out, Taylor and the 16-year-old actress visited the Eiffel Tower and went on the carousel at Montmartre.

On her return to the States, she poked fun at herself by announcing her real great love – Diet Coke. In a YouTube video, she said: 'I wanted to share some news with you, because we're finally making it official with one of the great loves of my life . . . Diet Coke.' She then showed off the famous silver-and-red can.

In a statement, she added: 'I've said for years that Diet Coke just "gets me" and my lifestyle. I'm so excited about our new partnership.' The ad later saw her compose the lyrics for her song '22', while sipping the cold drink and various other people joining in with the catchy song.

All the stars of the music world donned their best outfits for the Grammys at the start of February. As Taylor got ready in her dressing room, putting the finishing touches to her make-up, Ed Sheeran sat on the floor, playing his guitar, and the pair talked about Taylor's forthcoming tour. Sir Elton John also popped in to say 'Hi' and before she knew it, Taylor was back in the limelight.

After gliding down the red carpet in a J. Mendel dress, she sent a not-so-subtle message to ex-boyfriend Harry, as she performed the opening number, 'We Are Never Ever Getting Back Together', in a white top hat, tailcoat and hot pants. Halfway through the song, which saw her surrounded by a man riding a tricycle, a flame-thrower and a company of clowns, she broke into a deep British accent to say: 'So, he calls me up and says, "I still love you." But I said, "I'm sorry, I'm busy opening up the Grammys – and we're never, ever getting back together."' The audience went crazy.

With six Grammys under her belt already, this was one award she would never tire of being given and she showed just how thrilled she was to take home another trophy as she graced the stage as part of the pre-telecast section of the annual show in a sleeveless cream frock with silver-pattern detail and beige Christian Louboutin heels. She was visibly emotional as she put her head in her hands in front of the star-studded audience, closing her eyes as she digested her win for Best Song Written for Visual Media for 'Safe & Sound'. The awestruck look on her face remained as she watched every award – she was sincerely happy, shocked and surprised.

Later in February, she also managed to have another dig at Harry, while filming her new video for '22' in Malibu. Not only did she wear a knitted beanie hat like the one he religiously wore during their time together, but she also parodied some of their significant moments. In particular, she was seen running up to a friend to do a version of the *Dirty Dancing* lift – something she was famously said to have recreated with Harry near the start of their relationship.

The pair were going to come face to face again, at the high-profile BRIT Awards in London. When Harry was asked about Taylor during a London Fashion Week after-party, he told *Grazia* magazine: 'I'm not worried about seeing her at all. She's a sweet girl, you know, I don't have a bad word to say about her.'

However, according to reports, everything was being done to keep the pair away from each other and show bosses even organised for them to rehearse on separate days.

A backstage insider said: 'No one wants anything awkward to happen. Taylor and Harry are definitely being kept well apart . . . Taylor is near Robbie [Williams], Justin Timberlake, Mumford & Sons and James Corden in one area – Harry is down a different corridor with an extra-large room for himself and the other 1D lads. The 1D dressing room is well hidden, too, so if Taylor did want to find Harry and smooth things over, she'd have to do some serious looking before she'd find him.'

The night before the event, Taylor and Ed Sheeran sparked yet more romance rumours after they were holed up in a hotel room until 4 a.m., when Ed left looking 'very happy' and 'pleased with himself'.

He later explained to New Zealand broadcaster TVNZ: 'I did go to her hotel, I did stay there 'til four and I did leave in the same clothes. But I was playing her my new record. It was strictly that kind of thing. Literally, I went in there and we passed the guitar back and forth and played songs to each other.'

Asked whether he stole a kiss, he responded: 'I'm a professional . . . The thing that impressed me with the media is that because they wrote about it, my mates believed it. And my mates are texting me, being like, "Is it true?" So I said it wasn't but the fact that people can believe it makes me feel like a bit of a stud, you know? I've got to be honest because one of my best friends did date her. I'm not that kind of guy. But the fact that people believed it impressed me a little bit.'

On the night of the BRITs, Taylor was clearly out to impress and turned heads with another floor-length choice from Ellie Saab, with thigh-high sheer panels. After catching sight of her, Robbie Williams said she was 'really fit', before adding he was hoping he had a shot with her, saying: 'It'll be my go soon.'

The split was on everyone's minds. Sharon Osbourne, who presented the International Female Award alongside

Dermot O'Leary, said, as she took to the stage: 'Where is that little Harry Potter? Has he got his little magic stick here tonight – that's his willy!'. While James Corden poked fun at Harry's love of 'cougars', asking him who he was hoping to score with – and giving him the choice of 60-year-old Sharon or Annie Lennox.

Taylor put the ribbing aside for her performance of 'I Knew You Were Trouble', where she ditched her good-girl look for a far edgier and raunchier vibe, arriving on stage in a white floor-length gown, before stripping off to reveal a lacy black playsuit and knee-high boots. During the energetic routine, complete with pyrotechnics, a full band and dramatic dance routines, she thrust up against her male dancers.

Afterwards, when she was asked about the show-stopping performance by *The Times Magazine*, she confirmed, once and for all, the song was definitely about Harry, saying: 'Well, it's not hard to access that emotion when the person the song is about is standing by the side of the stage watching. You're balancing the analytical side of your brain, which is telling you where to go and how to go there, with the other side of your brain, which is saying, "Feel everything you're singing, and show it on your face. Feel everything exactly as you felt it when you wrote the song."'

Taylor also sat through 1D's rendition of 'One Way or Another (Teenage Kicks)'. Clearly, Harry had enjoyed the newer, sexed-up Taylor and, when he was cornered at the Sony after-party, he said: 'I thought her performance was really good. She looked great.'

Taylor also celebrated afterwards and was seen at the

Universal bash at Soho House, on the decks, alongside host James Corden, dancing with Rizzle Kicks' Jordan Stephens and chatting to actress Carey Mulligan and her husband Marcus Mumford.

The following morning, she was up bright and early, dressed in a pretty yellow dress, and continued on her whirlwind tour, which included a performance and interview on *The Graham Norton Show*.

She was also seen in a casual plaid shirt and flat shoes as she dined out in Soho with friends, including rising British singer Tom Odell. She had been seen talking to him at the Universal bash, and Tom, who had won the Critics' Choice Award at the BRITs, said Taylor was an 'incredible lyric-writer'. After dinner, the group moved on to the Groucho Club.

Afterwards, he told the *Guardian*: 'She's just a lovely 23-year-old girl. There's not really much more to it. I have to be careful what I say. That whole little escapade was, I don't know . . . It was very cool.'

After being asked time and time again about Harry, Taylor had had enough. She finally gave in to the demand and dished the dirt through an unnamed source to glossy magazine *Vanity Fair*. She wanted to have her say.

She admitted she couldn't trust the One Direction star after he kissed another girl in the early stages of their romance, suggesting that they did have a fling in April 2012. And even when 'he wore her down' – presumably at the end of the year – and Taylor gave him a second chance, she 'felt like he was looking at every girl.'

The source added: 'Then when they were in London, he disappears one night and after that it was like he just didn't want to keep going . . . It was like a pendulum for her, swinging back and forth. [Conor Kennedy was] just like a two-month thing [but Taylor] says he was awesome. She dated Jake [Gyllenhaal] and John [Mayer] when she was really young and they were in their thirties, and she got really hurt. So it was like, "That hurt – this won't. But then it did."'

She also ranted about being portrayed as clingy. She blasted: 'For a female to write about her feelings, and then be portrayed as some clingy, insane, desperate girlfriend in need of making you marry her and have kids with her, I think that's taking something that potentially should be celebrated – a woman writing about her feelings in a confessional way – that's taking it and turning it and twisting it into something that is frankly a little sexist.'

Taylor was determined to have the last word, and she did. The best revenge she could have against the media-sniping and her celebrity exes would be to master her transition from teen star to grown-up rock star with ease. She was managing that and a whole lot more. Her Red tour would show how accomplished she had become.

CHAPTER FOURTEEN

'You are the longest and best relationship I've had'

After hours of preparations and months of rehearsals, Taylor's highly anticipated Red tour brought the house down when it opened in Omaha, Nebraska, on 13 March.

Talking about the more sophisticated set, she told Taste of Country: 'The way I kinda look at this tour, from an aesthetic point of view, from the way the visuals are, I really think that my last two tours, if I were to pick a place where they would exist, it would be a fantasy world where there are princesses and fairies and castles. If this tour existed in a place, it would exist in a city. It's a glammed up vision of what I would wear every day. Or a rocked out version of what I would wear out at night.'

As in her previous tours, Taylor switched the songs up each night and did a number of covers of other artists' works, so no two nights were exactly the same. As normal, Andrea scouted the crowd for twenty to forty fans to be given passes for the singer's special T-Parties, in this case access to her 'Club Red', where they got to meet Taylor, Ed and the backing dancers and band after the shows.

Ed said: 'I'm loving it. I've been very fortunate with the tours that I've been invited on . . . I go there, hang out with Taylor, I play a show, do my duet with her, then I hang out a bit more and then I go. So, really, it's a nice tour.'

He added to E! Online: 'Six months is a long time to go on tour and leave your family and friends and if you haven't got a friend on the road it can get quite lonely.'

Taylor took a break from her tour to attend the Academy of Country Music Awards in Las Vegas on 7 April. Wearing a gold Dolce & Gabbana chainmail-style dress, she had nods for Entertainer of the Year, Female Vocalist of the Year, Album of the Year for *Red* and Video of the Year.

Taylor fulfilled her pledge from the previous year and took leukaemia survivor Kevin McGuire with her. His sister, Tori, posted pictures of them posing together, with the caption, 'The moment we have all been waiting for.' She added: 'It's great how this has all worked out, it truly came full circle; Kevin is fully healthy this year and will be able to enjoy everything!'

Despite the huge success of her album, surprisingly, Taylor walked away empty-handed but was praised for her performance with Tim McGraw and Keith Urban of 'Highway Don't Care'. Taylor's ex, John Mayer, also sang. *Us Weekly* claimed that Taylor 'demanded' to perform before him but the reports were quickly shot down by her rep. Afterwards, there were stories saying she was seen getting close to John at the aftershow party at the Orleans Hotel & Casino.

An insider told *Grazia* magazine: 'Taylor spotted John on the red carpet, but it was only at the party that they got talking. They snuck off to a corner and were all over each other. At one point she had her hands on his knees, with him holding her waist – they were so deep in conversation.'

It allegedly turned into an all-night reunion as Taylor invited John for breakfast at her hotel room but, again, the rumours were denied by her publicist, who said there was 'no truth in this . . . whatsoever.'

Taylor was naturally disappointed with her lack of wins but returned to the stage twenty-four hours later for Tim McGraw's Summer Night, held at the same venue as the previous night, the MGM Grand Garden Arena. Dressed in a clingy black Elizabeth & James number with sheer panels and strappy black John Michel Cazabat heels, Taylor gave a passionate performance, swinging the microphone and swishing her hair for another rendition of 'Highway Don't Care' with Tim and Keith.

By this point, Taylor had managed to put Harry Styles to the back of her mind, but sadly not for long. As Taylor headed back on tour, she was hit by claims that her ex had labelled her a 'pain in the arse' and said he was never serious about her.

According to the *Daily Star Sunday*, in One Direction's fly-on-the-wall documentary, *This Is Us*, Harry said: 'I haven't met a girl yet who I'd want to even think of getting serious with. I think I've been unlucky in love so far. But then, I haven't really met anyone who's made the earth move for me . . . I'm longing to meet someone who really inspires me and makes me really want to spend time with them.'

At the start of May, Taylor was back in the market for a new property and purchased a $17 million mansion on Rhode Island. Astonishingly, according to TMZ, she paid in one single transfer of cash. The 11,000-square-foot mansion was in the upmarket town of Watch Hill and had seven bedrooms, nine bathrooms and a huge circular driveway.

She moved in almost immediately with the help of her mum and dad – and included in her move was one of her most valued possessions: a chair where she does a lot of her songwriting. Not long afterwards, much to Taylor's dismay, an obsessed fan was arrested after trying to swim up to the house in a bid to meet her and she was forced to hire extra security to monitor the property round the clock.

Thankfully, she was away at the time, having ditched the music scene for a night devoted to fashion – the Costume Institute Gala at New York's Metropolitan Museum of Art (often known as the Met Ball), celebrating 'Punk: Chaos to Couture'. The starlet wore a stunning black J. Mendel dress with an ornate bejewelled collar, paired with punky pink streaks in her hair and vampish black nails.

Once inside the event, she caught up with Gwyneth Paltrow and Zooey Deschanel. Taylor and Zooey had become good friends and Taylor found time in her hectic schedule to flex her acting muscles opposite the brunette in the Season 2 finale of

Zooey's show, *New Girl*. Taylor played a woman called Elaine who was a surprise guest at the wedding.

Jake Johnson – who portrays Nick Miller in the show – jokingly complained that she handled her day on set like she had been doing it for years.

He said: 'She came in and is really nice. It's not an easy scene. There were probably 70 extras there – though I'm sure she performs to so much bigger [crowds] than that on a regular basis.' Zooey added: 'She's awesome. She's super-funny and really smart. Very professional and we loved working with her.'

Of course, there are always more awards shows to attend and, on 19 May, Taylor went to the *Billboard* Music Awards at the MGM Grand Garden Arena in Las Vegas. She matched the blue of the carpet in a glittering Zuhair Murad dress, paired with Jimmy Choo heels.

'Billboards? On ABC. You watching?' she tweeted.

Taylor really was the lady of the night at the end, scooping 8 out of her 11 nominations, including Top Artist, Top Female Artist, Top Digital Songs Artist and Top *Billboard* 200 Album for *Red*.

Her most memorable speech was for Artist of the Year, the big prize of the night, where she had beaten the likes of Justin Bieber and One Direction.

'I just want to thank you guys for making my music the soundtrack to your crazy emotions,' she said. 'You are the longest and best relationship I've had.'

Midway through the event, she performed '22' in a highly choreographed routine that saw her dancing on a table, leaping through a clothes rack, giving a high-five to Akon and then joining up with the *America's Best Dance Crew* champions, hip-hop dance crew the Jabbawockeez, and members of the Cirque du Soleil. At the end, hundreds of red balloons fell from the ceiling. Taylor was dressed in a playful ensemble of girly silver shoes, black high-waisted shorts and a unicorn T-shirt, adorned with the phrase HATERS GONNA HATE.

Afterwards, she partied with her best pal, Selena Gomez. 'It's so much fun especially when she's there,' Taylor said to E! TV. 'It sort of turns into a dance party situation and we don't like to think of these things as pressure, like, "Oh, my God, everybody's watching, how do you act?" We just act like we do in our kitchen. It was a blast.'

However, she was caught on camera backstage sticking her tongue out and grimacing when Selena kissed her ex, Justin on the cheek. With rumours the couple might get back together, Taylor clearly wasn't too thrilled at her friend's choice. When *Access Hollywood* asked what she and Selena were whispering about when Justin picked up his award, she apparently said: 'Oh, you do not want to know! You do not want to open that can of worms.'

Many artists had duetted with Taylor on her tour and a few days later she had the honour of singing with music legend Mick Jagger and the Rolling Stones live in Chicago. Performing a stripped-back version of 'As Tears Go By' on the band's 50 & Counting tour, Taylor wowed onlookers in a short playsuit with sheer lace sleeves.

Taylor admitted it was another career highlight, and one of

the best bits was backstage before the show. She told the *Daily Star*: 'One of my favourite moments of the whole day was when the musical director, Mick and I were rehearsing the song in a dressing room with a piano. We were goofing around and we started dancing and twirling around the room.'

Afterwards, she concluded: 'Performing with the Rolling Stones was everything that you think it would be and a bit better.'

Taylor loves switching up her look and, two days after-wards, attended the Country Music Television Awards back in Nashville with her brother Austin. She looked angelic on the red carpet in an ethereal cream dress, before she changed into a vampish black bustier and shorts with a red cape, to perform 'Red', and swished her hair and joined in with her bandmate for his guitar solo.

Despite walking away empty-handed and missing out on the coveted Video of the Year award, which Carrie Underwood won for 'Blown Away', Taylor seemed determined to have a fun night. Unlike lots of other buttoned-up stars, Taylor was seen dancing in the aisles, letting out a cheer as each win was announced and boogying away through other performances like no one was watching.

Nashville's finest then gathered for the CMA Music Festival and Taylor performed 'Highway Don't Care' with Tim McGraw and Keith Urban. 'Thank you @TheTimMcGraw & @KeithUrban for joining me onstage for 'High Way Don't Care' at CMA Fest!' Taylor tweeted. 'And thanks for the #1,country radio! FUN!'

Taylor's work ethic never wanes and she told reporters

before the event that she's ready to start working on new music.

'It's starting,' she said. 'All the anxiety is starting. When the anxiety starts, the writing happens right after, usually. Whatever I write in the first year is going to get thrown away. I'm going to like it, but it's going to sound like the last record. The second year usually sounds like the next project. I think you need to change up your influences. I think you need to be inspired by different things than you were inspired by before.'

Taylor will continue to play sell-out crowds across the globe in 2013 on her Red tour and no doubt will have many more chart-topping hits along the way. While she loves the life she has made for herself, music will still remain at the centre of her world, as it has done since she was a child growing up.

She told the *Philadelphia Inquirer*: 'I think anyone, when they come across something that fascinates them more than anything they've ever seen – and that's what music does for me – I think when each person finds that in their life, that's when they become driven. That's when they grow up. I was just kind of a fluke in that I found mine age 10. I was like: I found this. There's no way I can let it go.'

She says she finds it difficult to believe she's not dreaming her life and her emotions are not fake. As for her fans, ensuring their happiness is right at the top of her list of priorities.

'I love all the girls who have my songs on MySpace,' she declared. 'I love the people who come to my shows . . . I love the people at those shows who sing along with me. I love reading your stories in emails, some so touching they've given me chills. I love every single person, who has wanted my autograph, because for the life of me I never really thought it would mean something to someone for me to write my name down.'

She knows she will never have a normal life but she wouldn't change it for a second. Her dream did come true.

'Nothing in my life now, as far as activities and the way people perceive me, it's not normal and it's a lot different . . . It's better. I always dreamed about what it would be like if I would walk in somewhere and people already knew my songs, and it's crazy . . . It's amazing to me that it actually happened.'

Picture Credits